Basic Project Techniques

GENERAL PAINTING SUPPLIES

BRUSHES: 1″ Flat, synthetic; #14, #10, #8, #4 Flat, synthetic; #1 Liner and or striper, synthetic; #3 Round, synthetic; 1″ and 2″ Sponge brushes and ½″, ¾″ mop brushes.

PALETTE: **Permalba Artists' Acrylics:** Alizarin Crimson, Bright Red, Cadmium Red Light, Cadmium Yellow Medium, Hansa Yellow Light, Chrome Oxide Green, Cerulean Blue, Ultramarine Blue, Red Oxide, Yellow Ochre, Burnt Umber, Burnt Sienna, Paynes Gray, Mars Black, Titanium White, and Unbleached Titanium. **FolkArt Acrylics:** Barnwood, Persimmon, Cotton Candy, Thicket, Spanish Tile, and Apricot Cream. **Priscilla Hauser Acrylics:** Sunshine Gold, Malibu, and Autumn Rust. **Permalba Artists' Oils:** Burnt Umber, Burnt Sienna, Asphaltum, Raw Seinna, Ivory Black, Burnt Alizarin, Cadmium Orange, Cadmium Red Light, Ice Blue, Leaf Green, Leaf Green Dark, Naples Yellow, Permalba White, and Titanium White.

SUPPLIES: Wax paper palette, Palette knife, Tracing paper, Stylus, Paper towels, Fine and coarse grade of sandpaper, Container for water, Graphite and White transfer paper, Acrylic waterbase varnish, Old toothbrush, Odorless turpentine-Turpenoid, and Clear Acrylic Spray.

BACKGROUND PREPARATION

The design projects found in this book were all basically prepared in a similar way before painting with the exception of ***Heart Style.*** I prefer working on a primed background of gesso. Both acrylic and oil media work excellent on this type of surface finish. Follow this general procedure:

1. Lightly sand the given surface (wood or canvas) with a fine grade of sandpaper. Clean dust off.
2. Apply a coat of gesso to surface with a 1″ or 2″ sponge brush. Let dry.
3. Recoat surface with gesso, note if texture in background is desired, apply second coat in another direction (a weave look) or in all sorts of brush stroke directions (criss-cross look).
4. Allow surface to dry.
5. Transfer design using graphite paper.
6. Begin subject matter painting or trim out piece with desired base tone such as a color background. This background color may need to be applied before pattern transfer.

FINISHING

1. Allow painting to thoroughly dry before applying any type of finish. At least 48 hours after final oil glaze has been applied.
2. Using a 1″ sponge brush for a small object, a 2″ sponge brush for larger, smoothly coat entire piece with a waterbase or oil base varnish.
3. Note most waterbase varnishes will tend to beed up over oil colors. AquaTole waterbase varnish will properly work over oils. The proper, more durable and the finish to cause fewer problems over any mix media painting (acrylics with oils over) would be a high quality oil base varnish. Priscilla Hauser's Tole Finish is ideal.

TERMS

1. BASE - a tone applied in a color book style over the indicated area. Usually one to two coats of color will be needed for opaque coverage.
2. SHADE - indicates a tone or tones applied to the dark rendered areas of the painting. Refer to color photograph and ink design for placement of darks. Usually applied with a side loaded brush, always applied to a dry BASE tone.
3. HIGHLIGHT - is the brightest or lightest area of object. Sometimes it is necessary to build up to HIGHLIGHT area by painting gradual lighter tones up to lightest point. Can be accomplished with a dry brush technique, sand technique or side load technique.
4. ACCENT - is reflected color usually placed on an outer edge. An ACCENT will tie another color from the painting to a neighboring object.
5. OUTLINE and DETAIL - means to apply a strengthening line of color, usually a dark value, apply it with thin consistency paint using a liner brush. When outlining, allow breaks to occur on edge.
6. COLOR & COLOR - throughout the book multiple color names are mentioned, please note these differences: Bright Red *and* White - means using both colors in a given area but individually, *a mixture of* Bright Red and White - means mixing the two colors on the palette to achieve desired tone and value, Bright Red *plus* White - means the same as preceeding description.

TECHNIQUES

1. MIX MEDIA - Can be defined in several ways but as applied to the techniques in this book, means the application of a base of the acrylic

Basic Project Techniques

media then work is done on top with the oil media, hence the term MIX MEDIA. Note there is never an actual mixture of wet acrylic media with wet oil media. The oil media is placed over a dry acrylic media. One general rule to always follow: oils can be applied over acrylics but acrylics should never be applied over oils. The paintings found in this book have a base of acrylic work ie: base tone, some shading, and highlighting but they do heavily rely on oil glazes on top to finish shading tones and final contrast from light to dark.

2. DRY BRUSH - To create this technique a flat brush will be used with thick consistency paint. Pick up a flat brush that is thoroughly dry (no moisture) and load paint on the tip to lower edge of brush. Apply paint to surface with DRY BRUSH technique by lightly dusting the surface, applying color on just the top cross weaves of brush stroked base paint below.

3. SANDING - In my style of mix media, sanding becomes part of the painted technique. It is essentially used in the application of creating a HIGHLIGHT, but can achieve mid tones or worn weathered folk art effects. A medium to coarse sandpaper will be needed. Simply wrap paper around fingers and sand desired area to remove top color tones, allowing base tone to come through in places. Note: in order for this technique to be effective contrast is needed between base and top color tones in value, hue, and tone.

4. SIDE LOAD - To side load is the application of color to a flat brush. Side load means to carry one color or several colors on one side of a flat brush with corresponding medium on other (techniques in this book - medium for acrylic is water, oils is turp). Stroke moist brush along side pile of paint, pick up colors on one half, then blend on palette to soften colors. You should achieve strong color on one side that blends away into a transparent color wash to straight medium (a non-defining edge).

5. WASH -The paint is thinned with given medium to more than ink consistency. Paint is transparent enabling light to pass through, allowing base tone to show after application of color wash on top.

6. GLAZE - Paint is thinned to a very transparent consistency, pigment is maintained through the body of the medium. GLAZE should tint the surface.

7. ANTIQUE - Antiquing techniques can vary a great deal. The pieces in this book were antiqued in the oil media and in a heavy consistency and contrast oriented technique.

A. Use oil colors as they come from the tube, cream any excess oils into pigment if necessary. **B.** Moisten a 1″ sponge brush very slightly in turp. **C.** Stroke sponge brush through color or colors. **D.** Coat entire surface with thick color. **E.** Using soft paper towels wipe down piece to overall tone. **F.** Pick up soft tissues and begin wiping out HIGHLIGHT areas and mid tone areas, leave color tones in dark areas. **G.** Soften blending between tones with a mop brush.

8. BASECOAT - Apply BASE color tones in a smooth or coarse application (depending on desired effect ie: clean and sharp effect vs. rustic old effect). Simply fill in desired area with color or color mixture.

9. BRUSH SIZES - Brush size notations have not been made for given objects. My philosophy is always to use as large of a brush you can feel comfortable with. A larger brush will give you an effective look and faster results. The brush size is determined by the working size of the area.

10. LINER STROKES - As applied in ***Euro Style's European Floral*** design. It is a stroke development of tones through the use of a liner brush. Very thin hair like strokes of color are brushed in following the natural shape of the object. Thin consistency paint is essential in achieving this technique.

11. LINEWORK - A high quality liner brush is vital in rendering consistent linework. Paint should be thinned to an ink like consistency. Fully load brush in paint and twirl brush to form a point. Paint should easily flow from the tip of brush.

12. STRIPING - Can be accomplished with several tools, striper brush, liner brush, script liner brush or a ruling pen. ***Man Style's Country Harvest*** strict design feel required the use of letter perfect striping accomplished with a ruling pen. **A.** Thin paint to a flowing ink like consistency using proper medium. **B.** Open ruling pen to desired thickness and load paint by sliding a round brush full of paint on edge of slot area. **C.** Wipe outside edges of pen and test making some lines on palette surface. **D.** If paint does not release one or more of these steps can be followed: close pen opening, thin paint to a looser consistency, or touch tip with finger to help pull paint out. **E.** When you are ready to begin striping with ruling pen, be sure to use a raised ruler, preventing any seepage to occur.

Paintings with free form quality to them do not need the use of a ruling pen. ***Farm Style*** or ***Christmas Style*** projects evoke a folk art effect which striping can be accomplished with a striper brush through a looser less consistent manner. Also, note that these folk art projects are sanded for worn weather look resulting in a lesser need for perfect striping. Just keep in mind to thin paint down to a flowing consistency and fully load the brush.

Good luck! May these project techniques help you in developing your own PAINTING STYLE!

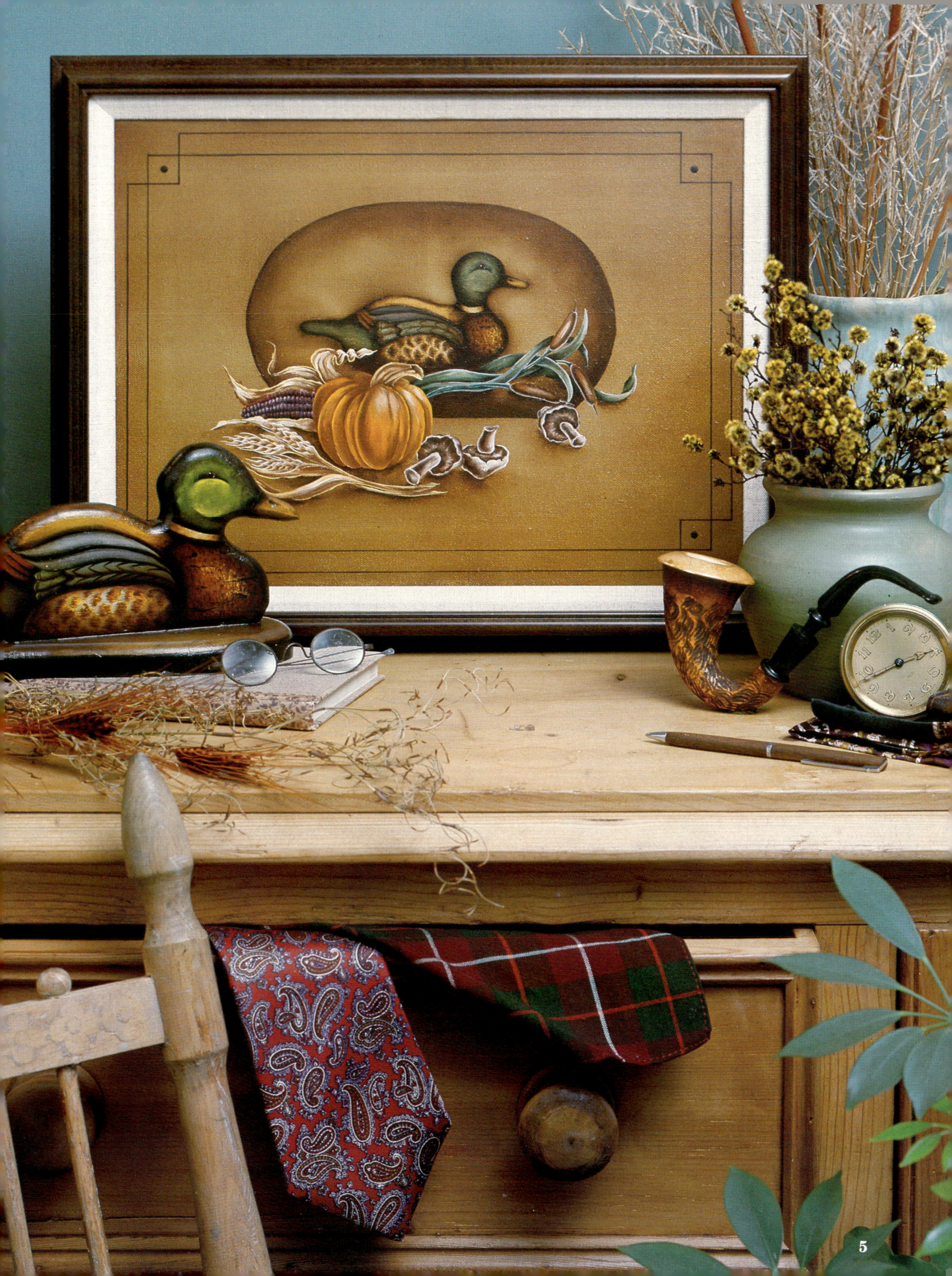

Mav STYLE

COUNTRY HARVEST

SURFACE: 12″ x 16″ stretched smooth canvas.

PALETTE: **Permalba Artists' Acrylics:** Burnt Sienna, Burnt Umber, Cadmium Yellow Medium, Mars Black, Red Oxide, Titanium White, Ultramarine Blue, Hookers Green, and Yellow Ochre.
Permalba Artists' Oils: Burnt Alizarin, Burnt Sienna, Burnt Umber, Cadmium Orange, Cadmium Red Light, Ice Blue, Ivory Black, Leaf Green, Leaf Green Dark, Naples Yellow, Permalba White, and Prussian Blue.

PAINTING INSTRUCTIONS

A. BACKGROUND: *Acrylics/Oils*
1. Basecoat entire canvas with Malibu acrylic. Let dry.
2. Apply a second coat of Malibu and lightly sand when dry. An opaque coverage is desired.
3. Apply a light stain of Burnt Umber oil color over canvas surface. Thin color with Turpenoid to stain. Let dry.
4. Trace and transfer design onto canvas using white transfer paper.
5. Place oval shape on with Burnt Umber oil color. Blend with mop brush.

B. DUCK DECOY: *Acrylics*
1. The duck decoy is mainly painted in acrylics with a few oil glazes on top. Each section is broken down into: a. BASE: tone applied in a color book style over the area. b. SHADE: tone or tones applied with a SIDE LOADED brush. c. HIGHLIGHT - color tone is applied with a DRY BRUSH technique. d. ACCENT - reflected color usually placed on outer edge.
2. Section 1 is painted in a BASE mixture of Hookers Green plus Black. Shade with Mars Black. Highlight with a mixture of Yellow Ochre plus White.
3. Section 2 is painted in a BASE mixture of Cadmium Yellow Medium. SHADE with Burnt Sienna. Hightlight with a mixture of Cadmium Yellow Medium plus White.
4. Section 3 is painted in a BASE mixture of Titanium White. SHADE with a mixture of Mars Black and Burnt Umber.
5. Section 4 is painted in a BASE of Red Oxide. SHADE individually with Burnt Umber, Burnt Sienna, and Mars Black. Highlight with Cadmium Yellow Medium.
6. Section 5 is painted in a BASE mixture of Yellow Ochre plus Titanium White. SHADE with Burnt Sienna. Highlight with a mixture of Titanium White plus Yellow Ochre.
7. Section 6 is painted in a BASE mixture of Ultramarine Blue plus Titanium White plus Mars Black. SHADE with Mars Black.
8. Section 7 is painted in a BASE mixture of Yellow Ochre plus Viridian. SHADE with a mixture of Burnt Sienna plus Burnt Umber. Highlight with Yellow Ochre.
9. Section 8 is painted in a BASE mixture of Titanium White plus Yellow Ochre plus Burnt Sienna. Shade individually with Burnt Umber then Burnt Sienna.
10. Section 9 is painted in a BASE mixture of Ultramarine Blue plus Titanium White plus Burnt Umber. SHADE with Mars Black.
11. Section 10 is painted in a BASE of Red Oxide. SHADE with a mixture of Burnt Umber plus Mars Black.
12. Section 11 is painted in a BASE mixture of Hookers Green plus Mars Black. SHADE with a mixture of Burnt Umber plus Mars Black. HIGHLIGHT with a mixture of Yellow Ochre plus Titanium White.
13. SHADE entire decoy sections with a GLAZE of Burnt Umber and Ivory Black oil colors.

C. STILL LIFE ELEMENTS: *Acrylics/Oils*
The remaining still life elements are basecoated in Titanium White acrylic allowed to dry and then painted in oil colors.

D. CATTAILS: *Oils*
1. BASE in Burnt Sienna entire cattail except HIGHLIGHT area.
2. SHADE cattail with a mixture of Burnt Umber and Ivory Black.
3. Work up to a HIGHLIGHT area separately with the following colors: Cadmium Red Light, Cadmium Orange, and Permalba White.
4. Side load with Ice Blue and place an ACCENT on the right hand side.

E. CATTAIL BLADES: *Oils*
1. Cattail blades are painted with a BASE of Leaf Green and/or Leaf Green Dark.
2. They are shaded with Ivory Black, a little Prussian Blue, and Burnt Umber separately.
3. HIGHLIGHT and ACCENT with Ice Blue.

F. MUSHROOMS: *Oils*
1. BASE in Permalba White.
2. SHADE separately with Burnt Sienna and Burnt Umber.
3. HIGHLIGHT with Titanium White.

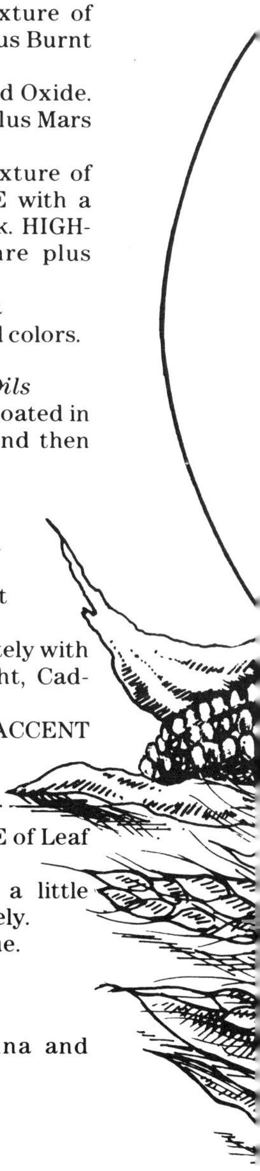

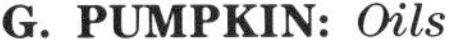

G. PUMPKIN: *Oils*
1. Apply Cadmium Orange as a BASE over entire pumpkin.
2. Using the following colors: Burnt Alizarin, Burnt Sienna, and Burnt Umber, place SHADE tones.
3. HIGHLIGHT with Naples Yellow and Permalba White.

H. PUMPKIN STEM: *Oils*
1. Base stem in Naples Yellow.
2. Burnt Sienna and Burnt Umber are used to SHADE with on the stem.
3. HIGHLIGHT with Titanium White.

I. CORN: *Oils*
1. BASE in Burnt Alizarin.
2. Corn kernals are individually shaded with Burnt Umber and Ivory Black.
3. HIGHLIGHT with Ice Blue and Titanium White.

J. CORN STOCK: *Oils*
1. Base in Naples Yellow.
2. SHADE with Burnt Sienna and a slight touch of Burnt Umber.
3. Titanium White is placed on as HIGHLIGHT.

K. WHEAT: *Oils*
1. Wheat is painted in a BASE of Naples Yellow.
2. Shade with Burnt Sienna.
3. Titanium White is used as a HIGHLIGHT.

L. GLAZING: *Oils*
When dry, glaze the still life in combinations of Burnt Umber, Burnt Sienna, and Ivory Black oil colors.

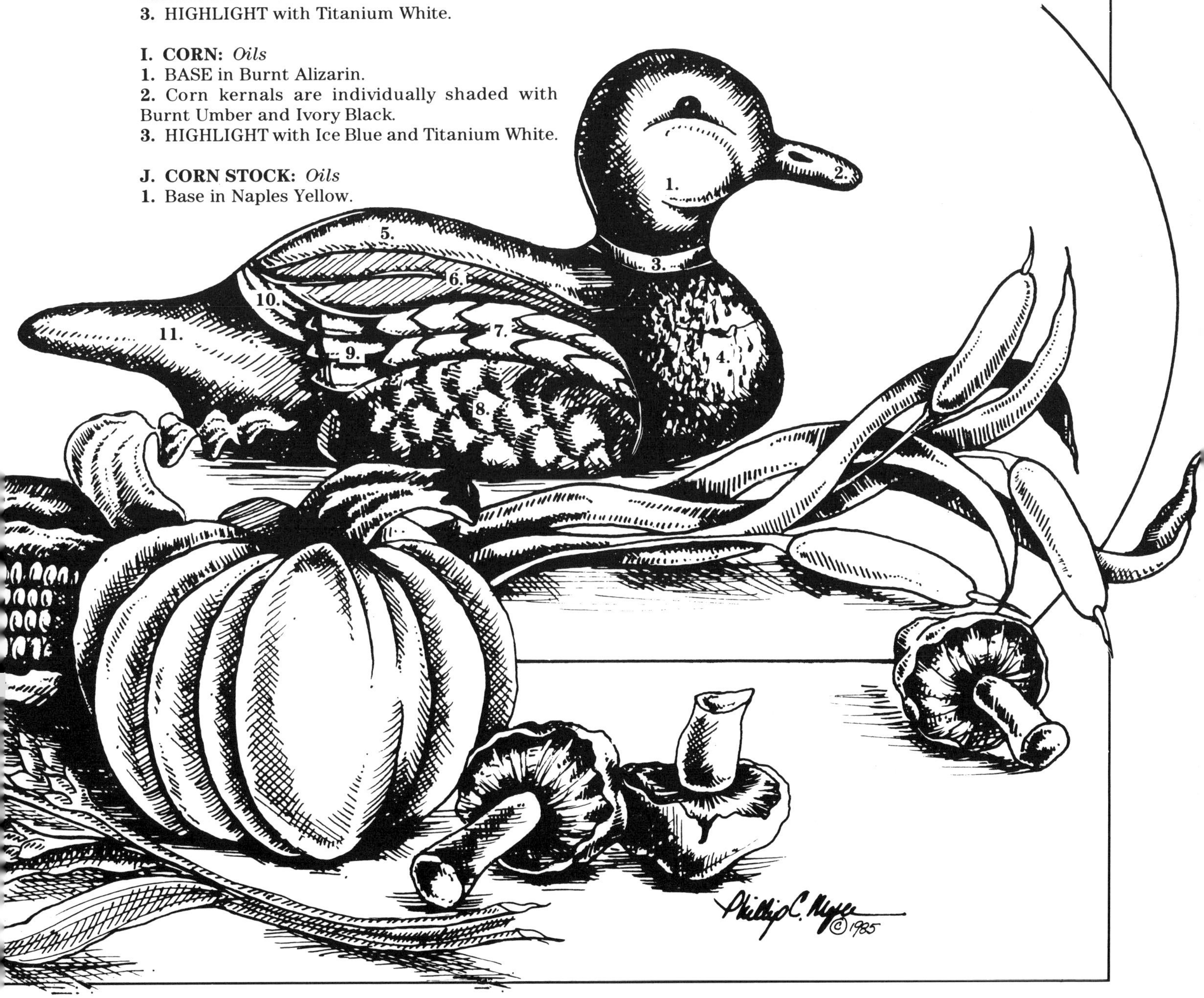

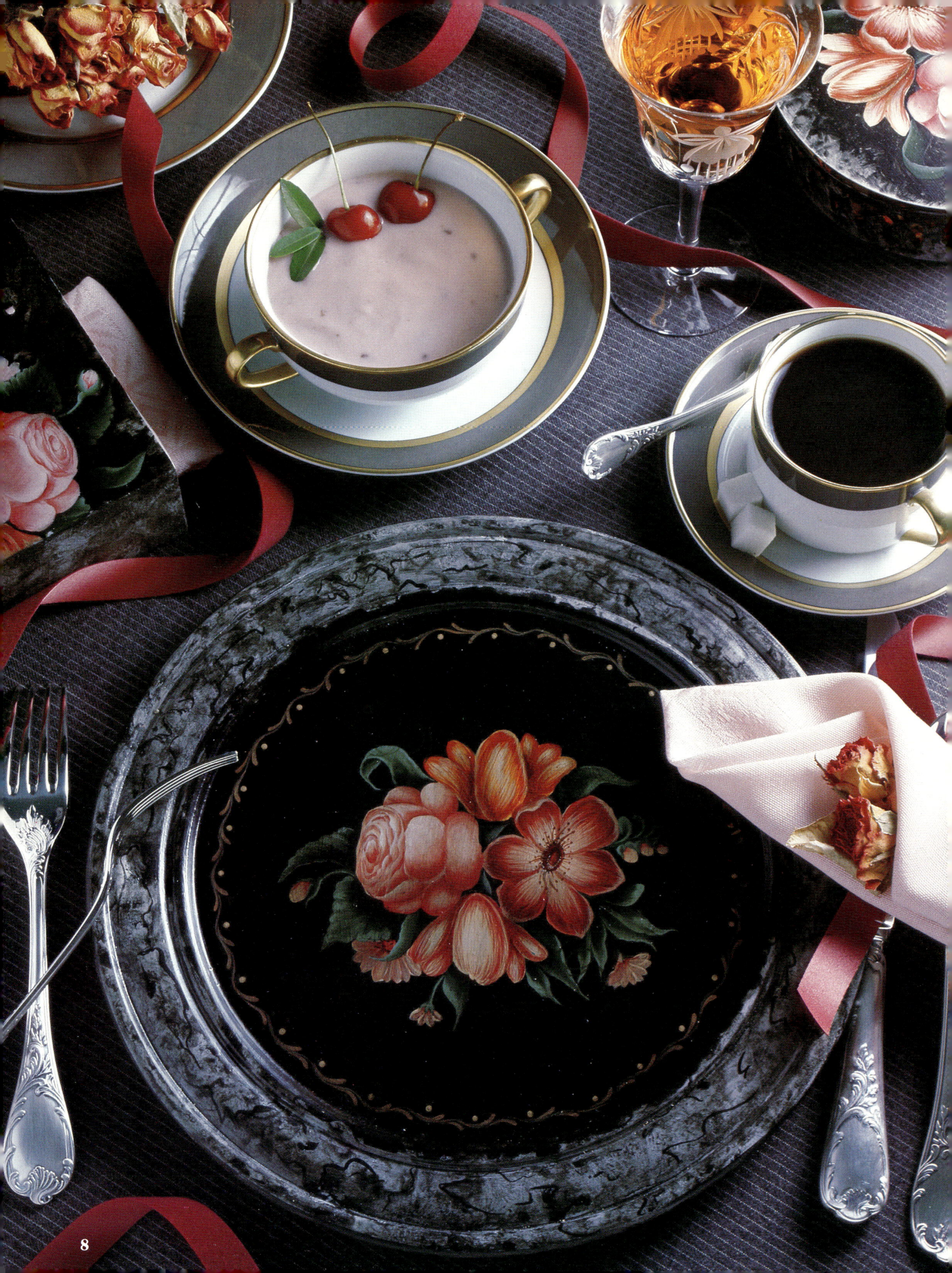

*Euro*STYLE

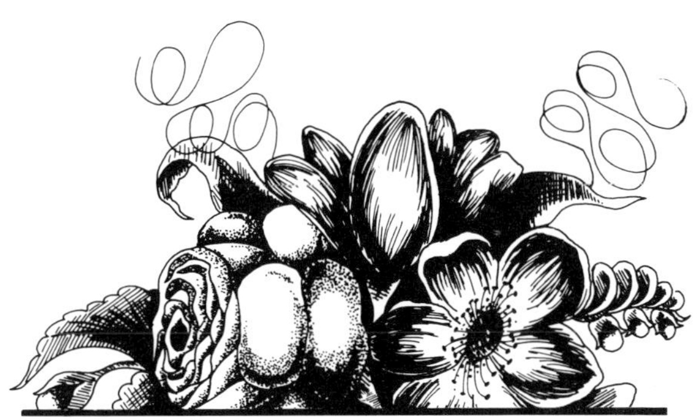

EUROPEAN FLORAL

SURFACE: 11½″ wooden plate.

PALETTE: **Permalba Artists' Acrylics:** Titanium White, Alizarin Crimson, Burnt Umber, and Ultramarine Blue. **FolkArt Acrylics:** Persimmon, Cotton Candy, Thicket, Spanish Tile, and Apricot Cream. **Permalba Artists' Oils:** Ivory Black.

PAINTING INSTRUCTIONS

A. BACKGROUND: *Acrylics*
1. Basecoat entire plate with gesso. Let dry. Apply a second coat.
2. Sand lightly and trace and transfer design.
3. **NOTE:** Black background color is painted after design is complete. Painting on the white background creates this stunning contrast and elluminousity.

B. CABBAGE ROSE: *Acrylics*
1. BASE rose shape in Cotton Candy.
2. Place a wash tone of Alizarin Crimson in dark areas.
3. SHADE by strengthening dark areas with a mixture of Alizarin Crimson plus Burnt Umber.
4. HIGHLIGHT with Cotton Candy plus Titanium White.
5. ACCENT with Titanium White.

C. ORANGE DUTCH TULIP: *Acrylics*
1. BASE top tulip in Cotton Candy. Let dry.
2. Overcoat BASE in Persimmon.
3. SHADE with liner strokes with a mixture of Alizarin Crimson.
4. Strengthen liner strokes with a mixture of Alizarin Crimson plus Burnt Umber.
5. ACCENT with Cotton Candy on edges.
6. HIGHLIGHT with Cotton Candy plus Persimmon and Cotton Candy plus Titanium White.

D. PINK DUTCH TULIP: *Acrylics*
1. BASE bottom tulip in Apricot Cream.
2. SHADE with liner strokes of Alizarin Crimson.
3. Strengthen with liner strokes of Alizarin Crimson plus Burnt Umber.
4. HIGHLIGHT with Apricot Cream plus Titanium White.

E. BLOSSOM: *Acrylics*
1. BASE in Spanish Tile.
2. SHADE with liner strokes of Alizarin Crimson plus Burnt Umber. Strengthen with Alizarin Crimson plus Burnt Umber. Strengthen with Alizarin Crimson plus Black.
3. Place lights on with a mixture of Spanish Tile plus Titanium White.

F. BLOSSOM CENTER: *Acrylics*
1. BASE center in Alizarin Crimson.
2. SHADE with a mixture of Alizarin Crimson plus Burnt Umber.
3. Paint stamen with thin curving lines of Burnt Umber plus Alizarin Crimson.
4. Paint loose dots for pollen in the following colors: Burnt Umber, Black, and Cotton Candy.

G. BUDS: *Acrylics*
1. BASE buds in Cotton Candy.
2. SHADE with an Alizarin Crimson wash.

H. DAISY & BUD: *Acrylics*
1. BASE petals in Cotton Candy.
2. Overstroke BASE with a brush loaded with Alizarin Crimson plus Burnt Umber tipped in Cotton Candy.
3. BASE daisy center in Alizarin Crimson.
4. Paint pollen in Burnt Umber.

I. LEAVES: *Acrylics*
1. BASE all leaves in Thicket.
2. Side load with Black and SHADE leaves.
3. HIGHLIGHT with a mixture of Thicket plus Titanium White plus Ultramarine Blue.

J. DETAIL: *Acrylics*
1. After design is completed, neatly and carefully outline entire design with a black line around design edge.
2. Coat black out from center area, allowing paint to become thinner and more transparent as the outer edge is approached.
3. The entire edge of the plate is nothing more than a Black wash dabbed here and there to create an abstract marble like pattern.
4. Create detail lines on marble edge with Black and a liner brush.
5. Brush stroke design is painted in Spanish Tile.

K. GLAZING: *Oils*
Place a glaze of Ivory Black over entire plate surface. SHADE and blend with a mop brush.

Euro STYLE
Phillip C. Myer ©1986

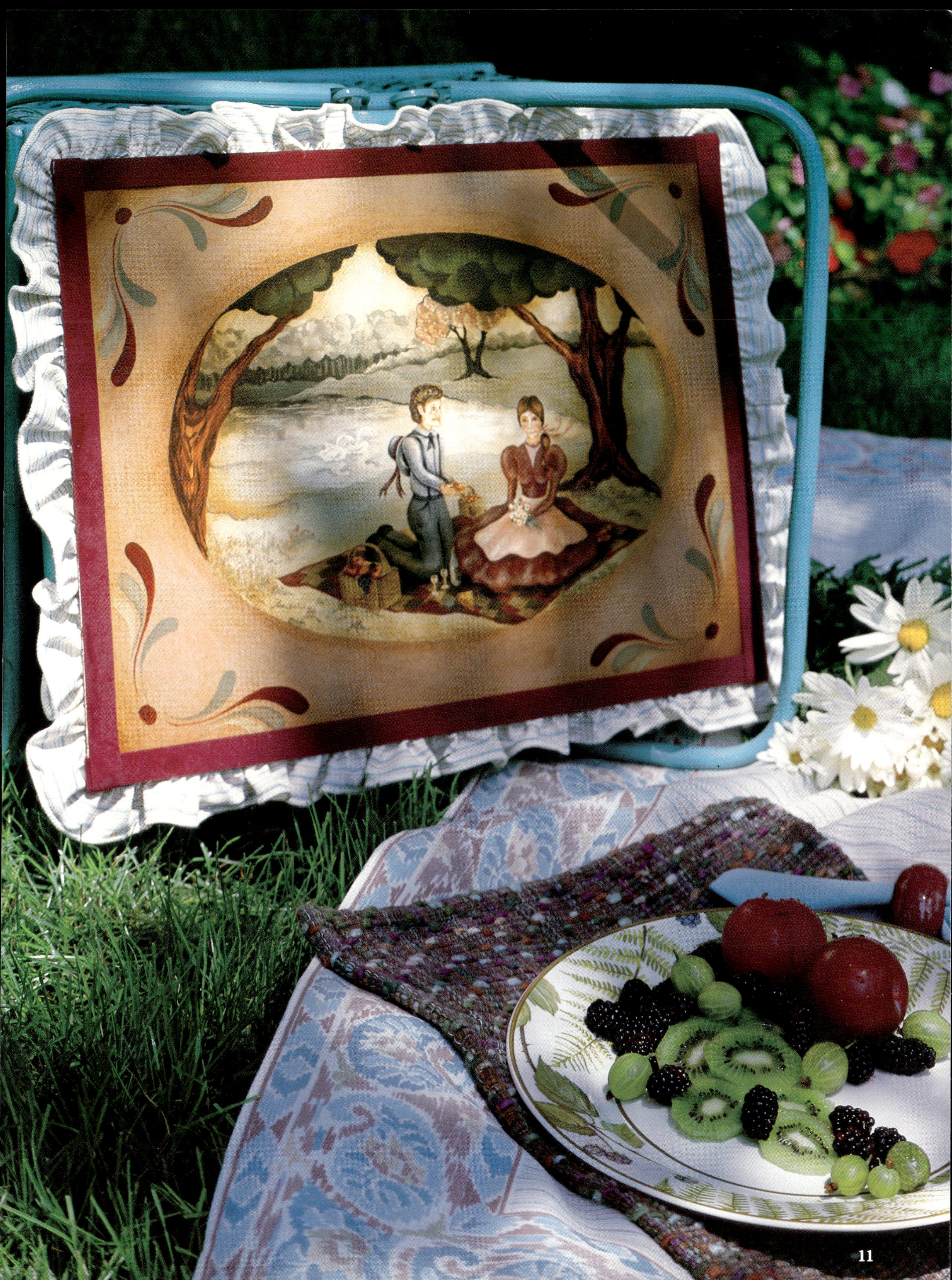

Picnic STYLE

A LOVER'S RENDEZVOUS AT SWAN POINT

Original in the collection of Caroline and Anthony Myer.

This project was originally featured in ***The Decorative Painter*** (July/August 1985 issue), a publication of the National Society of Tole and Decorative Painters, Inc.

SURFACE: 16¾″ x 12¾″ mounted canvas

PALETTE: **Permalba Artists' Acrylics:** Burnt Sienna, Burnt Umber, Alizarin Crimson, Mars Black, Cadmium Red Light, Titanium White, Chrome Oxide Green, Cadmium Orange, Cobalt Blue, and Yellow Ochre. **Permalba Artists' Oils:** Asphaltum, Burnt Umber, and Burnt Sienna.

PAINTING INSTRUCTIONS

A. BACKGROUND: *Acrylics*
1. Prepare canvas to fit given picnic basket by mounting canvas to a piece of illustration board, glue with permanent adhesive.
2. Coat canvas with gesso to seal. Let dry and sand lightly.
3. Trace and transfer the design. Apply only oval image and scene within.

B. SKY: *Acrylics*
1. BASE sky area in a mixture of Titanium White plus Cobalt Blue plus a touch of Chrome Oxide Green plus a very small amount of Cadmium Red Light.
2. Create a lighter shade of the above mixture and HIGHLIGHT center area of sky.

C. BACKGROUND TREES: *Acrylics*
1. Apply a BASE tone to trunk line area in a mixture of Chrome Oxide Green plus Cobalt Blue and a touch of Alizarin Crimson.
2. HIGHLIGHT between tree trunks with above mixture plus Titanium White.
3. Create tree top color by adding more White to the above mixture.
4. HIGHLIGHT tree tops with dry brushed Titanium White.

D. BACKGROUND BUSHES: *Acrylics*
1. Add more Chrome Oxide Green and Alizarin Crimson to the tree top mixture, brush this on the bush area.
2. SHADE at the base line with Cobalt Blue.

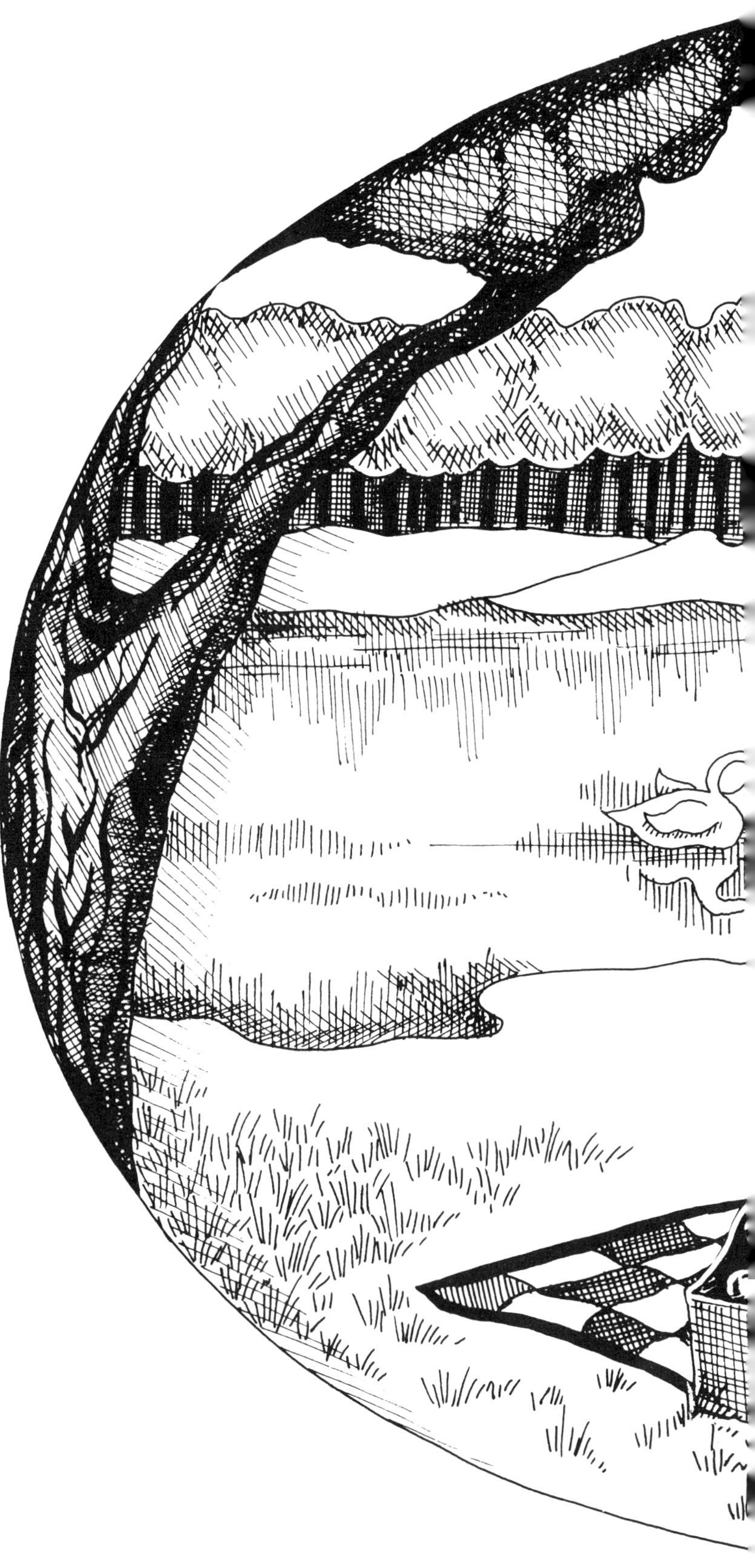

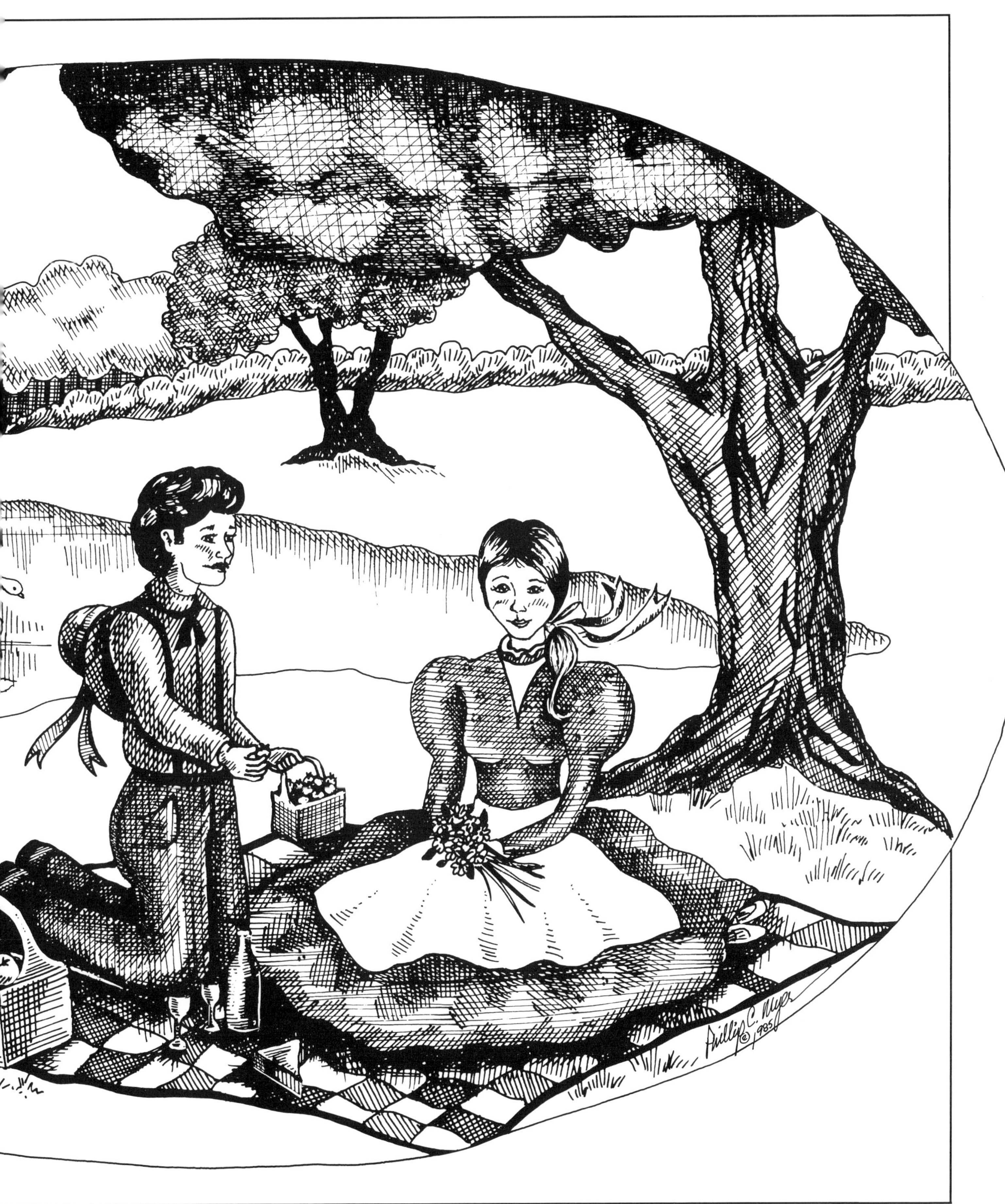

Picnic STYLE

3. HIGHLIGHT bushes with a dry brush of Chrome Oxide Green and White on edges.

E. LAND MASSES: *Acrylics*
1. Create three shades of green with Chrome Oxide Green plus Cobalt Blue plus Mars Black.
2. Apply darker values in the land masses in the background.
3. As the land masses approach the front areas, lighter values should be applied.

F. WATER AREA: *Acrylics*
1. BASE water in a mixture of Titanium White plus Cobalt Blue, a touch of Chrome Oxide Green.
2. Apply dark value of green mixture for reflection area in water.
3. Add White to blue mixture and dry brush strokes for water movement.

G. SWAN: *Acrylics*
1. BASE Swan in Titanium White.
2. SHADE with a mixture of Cobalt Blue plus Titanium White.
3. Drybrush the reflection in water area. ACCENT reflections with dark blue wash.
4. Paint eyes and beaks in Mars Black.

H. TREES: *Acrylics*
1. BASE the one background tree trunk in Green plus Cobalt Blue plus Black.
2. BASE its tree top in Green plus White.
3. ACCENT with a mixture of Alizarin Crimson plus Titanium White.
4. The two foreground tree trunks are BASED in a light wash of Burnt Sienna.
5. SHADE with stronger Burnt Sienna washes side loaded.
6. ACCENT with Black plus Burnt Umber markings.
7. BASE tree tops in dark green mixture.
8. ACCENT tree tops with "C" like strokes with lighter value green.

I. COUNTRY QUILT: *Acrylics*
1. The quilt is painted in patches of a light green, a dark green and a middle value burgundy.
2. SHADE with a Mars Black wash.

J. THE YOUNG LADY: *Acrylics*
1. BASE face in a flesh mixture. SHADE and detail with Burnt Sienna and Black.
2. Hair is painted in a Burnt Sienna wash, SHADE and detail with Burnt Sienna and Black.
3. BASE dress in a mixture of Alizarin Crimson plus Titanium White plus Burnt Umber. SHADE with a darker value, HIGHLIGHT with a lighter value by dry brushing.
4. Apron is painted in a light pink mixture made of dress mixture plus White. Dry brush White HIGHLIGHTS.

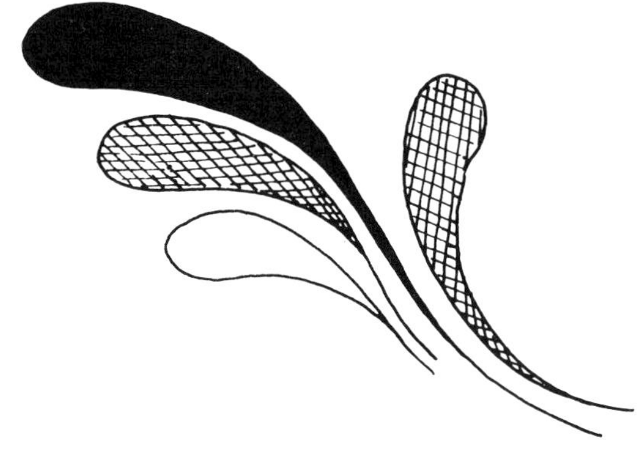

K. THE YOUNG MAN: *Acrylics*
1. BASE face in flesh mixture. SHADE and detail with Burnt Sienna and Black.
2. Hair is painted in a Burnt Umber wash, SHADE with Black.
3. BASE hat and pants in a mixture of Chrome Oxide Green plus Cobalt Blue plus Titanium White plus Mars Black.
4. BASE shirt in a lighter value of the above mixture. SHADE with Black, HIGHLIGHT with a dry brush of Titanium White.
5. Paint detail areas in Black, HIGHLIGHT in White.

L. PICNIC ELEMENTS: *Acrylics*
1. BASE baskets and slice of pie in Yellow Ochre, SHADE and detail in Burnt Sienna.
2. Fruits are based in various colors. SHADE with a Burnt Umber wash. HIGHLIGHT with White.
3. Wine bottle and glasses, BASE in White, SHADE with Burnt Umber and light green mixture.
4. Daisies are painted in White, Cadmium Yellow, and various green mixtures.

M. DETAILS: *Acrylics*
Brush strokes are painted with the three values of green and deep Alizarin mixture.

N. GLAZING: *Oils*
1. GLAZE all dark areas of design with a side loaded Black oil color. Let dry.
2. ANTIQUE entire piece in a mixture of Burnt Umber, Burnt Sienna, and a touch of Black oil colors.

O. FINISHING:
Trim with desired ribbon and fabrics.

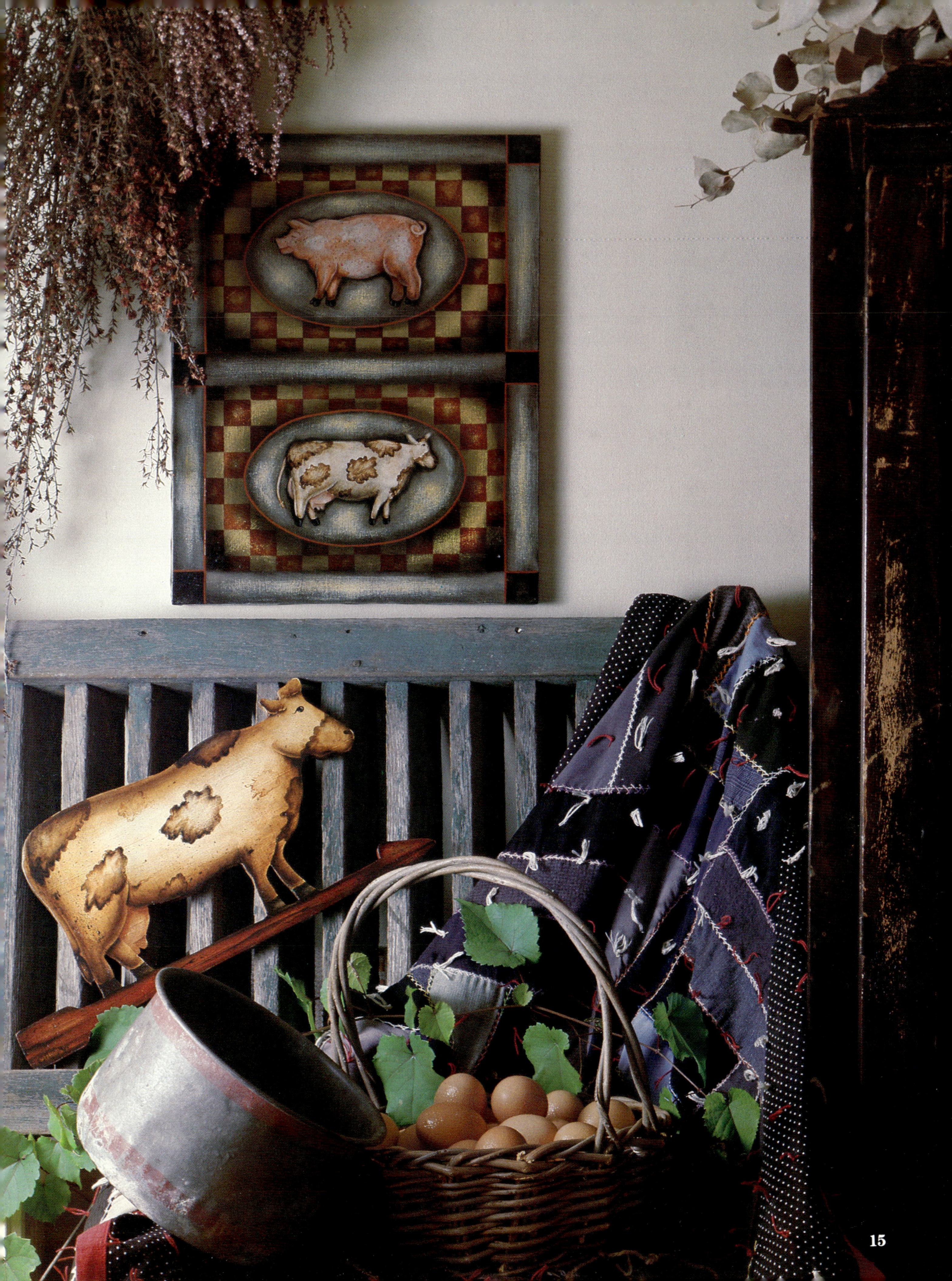

Farm STYLE

COUNTRY FARM CHECKERBOARD

SURFACE: 14″ x 18″ canvas and 16½″ x 8″ wood cut out.

PALETTE: **Permalba Artists'Acrylics:** Titanium White, Red Oxide, Alizarin Crimson, Burnt Sienna, Burnt Umber, and Unbleached Titanium. **FolkArt Acrylic:** Barnwood. **Priscilla Hauser Acrylics:** Sunshine Gold and Autumn Rust. **Permalba Artists' Oils:** Ivory Black and Raw Sienna.

PAINTING INSTRUCTIONS

A. BACKGROUND: *Acrylics*
1. Basecoat entire canvas and cut out with gesso. let dry.
2. Sand lightly and coat entire surface with Sunshine Gold acrylic.
3. Mark off 1¼″ border around canvas edge with pencil and ruler, then measure off a rectangle 7″ high x 11⅜″ wide for pig area then the1¼″ for middle border, leaving another 7″ high rectangle block for the cow.
4. Trace and transfer pig, cow, and checker designs. Note checker pattern only shows partial design. Continue checkers to fit 11⅜″ x 7″ rectangle and thick black rule to form oval.
5. Paint around pig and cow in the ovals and border strips with Barnwood acrylic.
6. Corner blocks are painted in Autumn Rust.
7. Oval checks are painted in Autumn Rust.
8. Once all background painting is dry, sand HIGHLIGHT in all areas. Center areas of all sections. Allow underneath base tones to come through.

B. PIG: *Acrylics*
1. BASE entire pig body in a mixture of Titanium White plus Alizarin Crimson plus Red Oxide.
2. SHADE with Red Oxide and Burnt Sienna.
3. Create pig markings with a wash of White. Also dry brush HIGHLIGHT with White.
4. Feet BASE in Mars Black, HIGHLIGHT in Titanium White.
5. Place mouth and eye detail on with Burnt Sienna.
6. Cut a simple mask (stencil like) to block surface around pig and flyspeck pig with Red Oxide, Burnt Sienna, and Burnt Umber.
7. SHADE around pig in oval area with a side loaded brush of Black.

C. COW: *Acrylics*
1. BASE cow shape in Unbleached Titanium.
2. SHADE body shape in Burnt Umber.
3. Apply a second wash of Burnt Sienna for shading.
4. BASE utters in pig pink mixture.
5. SHADE utters with Red Oxide and Burnt Sienna. HIGHLIGHT with White.
6. Paint cow markings on with a Burnt Umber wash side loaded.
7. Strengthen marks with a Mars Black wash.
8. Paint hoofs, eye, nose, and mouth features in Mars Black. HIGHLIGHT with Titanium White.

D. GLAZING: *Oils*
1. Side load a flat brush with Black oil color and place on the dark areas in the cow and pig. Blend with a mop brush to soften. Let dry.
2. Glaze entire piece with Black oil color and SHADE border areas.

E. DETAILS: *Oils*
Stripe oval and side border panels with Raw Sienna oil color.

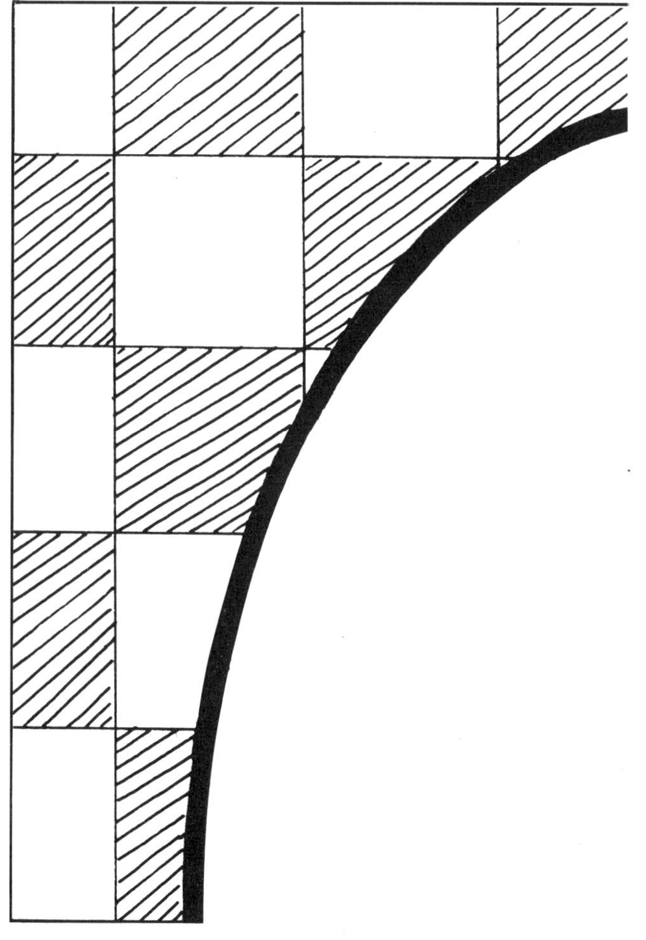

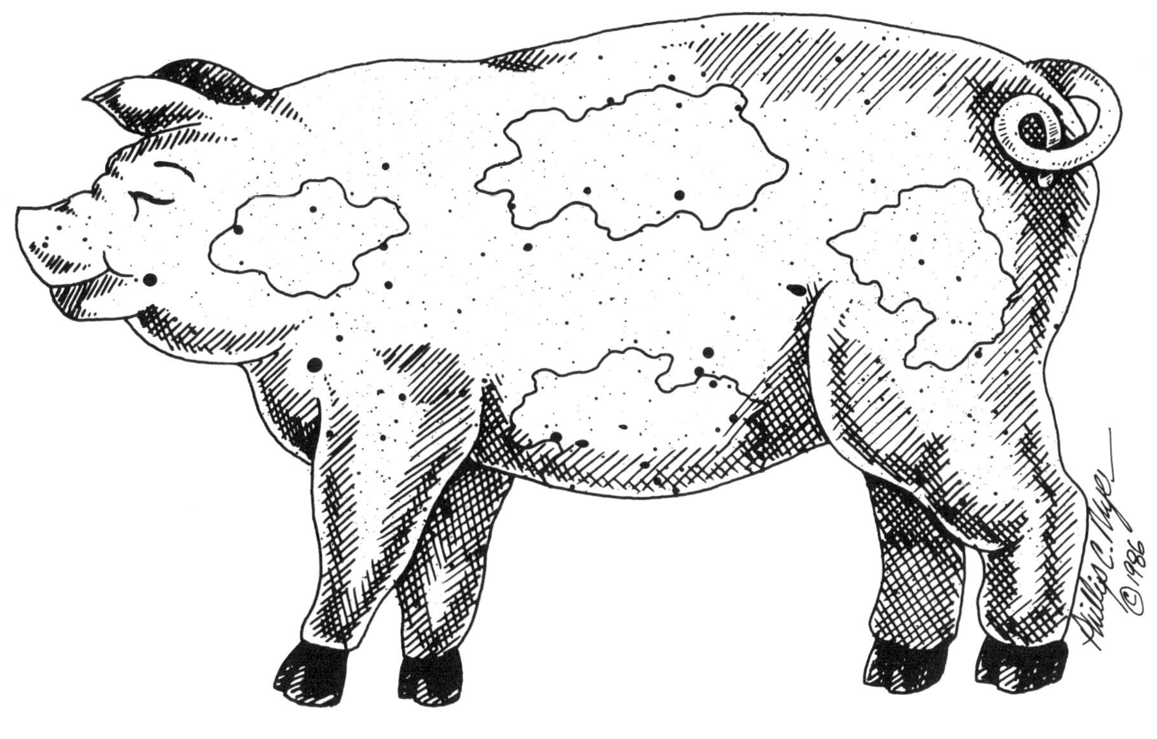

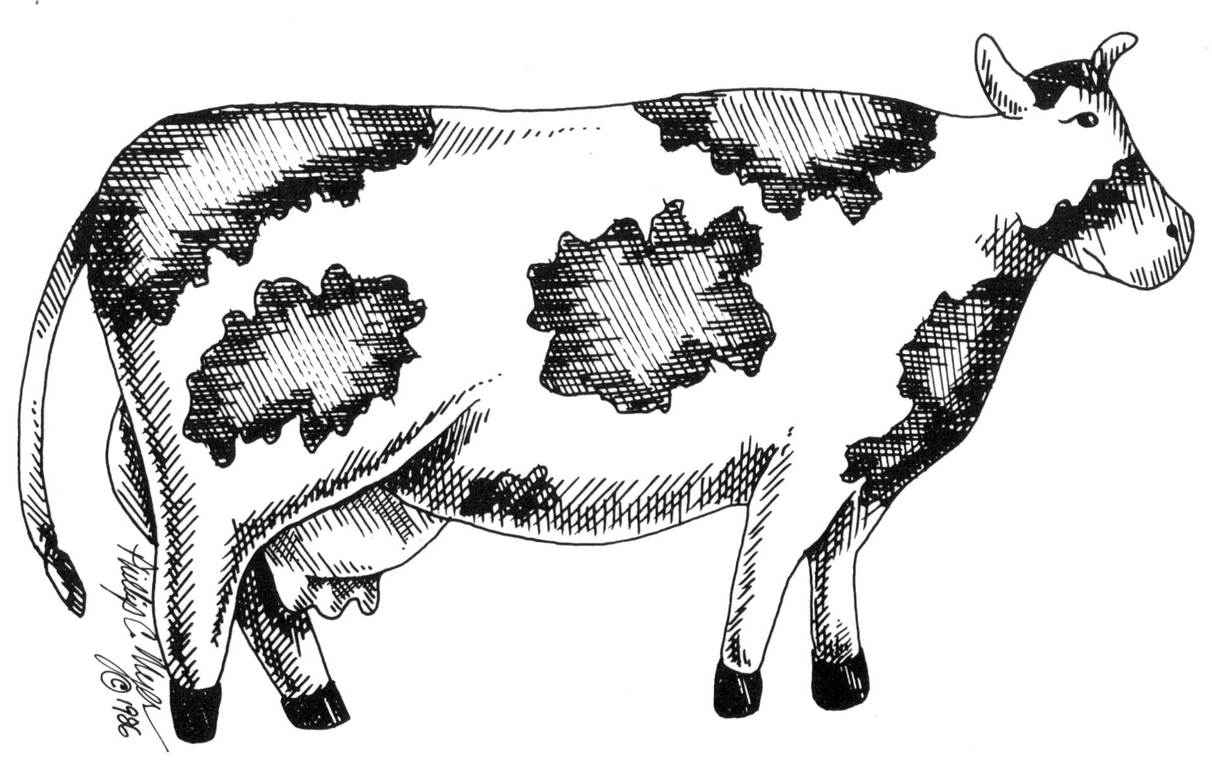

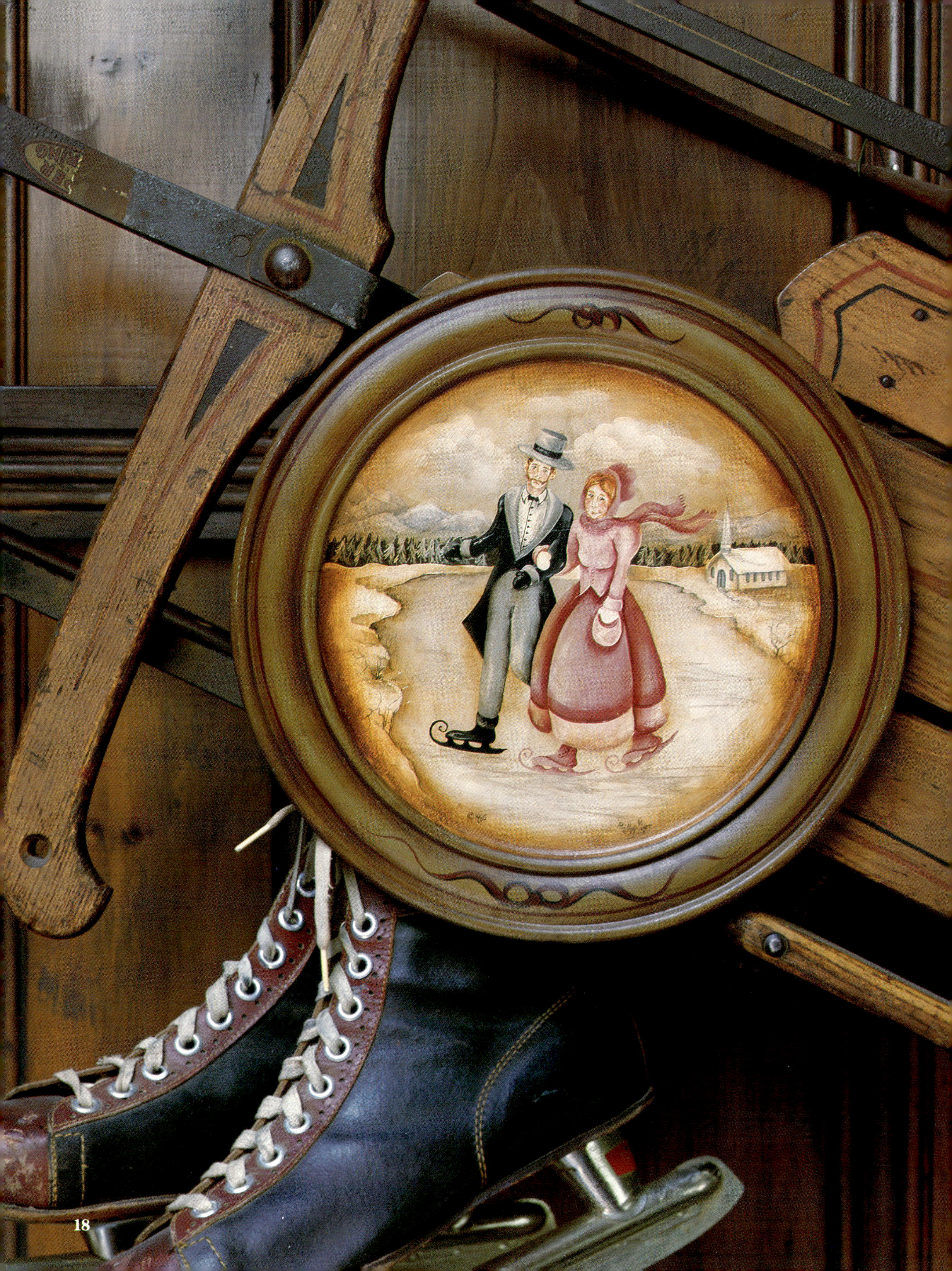

Winter STYLE

VICTORIAN SKATERS

Original in the collection of Christine Myer

SURFACE: 11½″ wooden plate.

PALETTE: **Permalba Artists' Acrylics:** Titanium White, Chrome Oxide Green, Paynes Gray, Mars Black, Burnt Sienna, Cadmium Red Light, Alizarin Crimson. **Priscilla Hauser Acrylic:** Cornflower Blue. **Permalba Artists' Oil:** Burnt Umber.

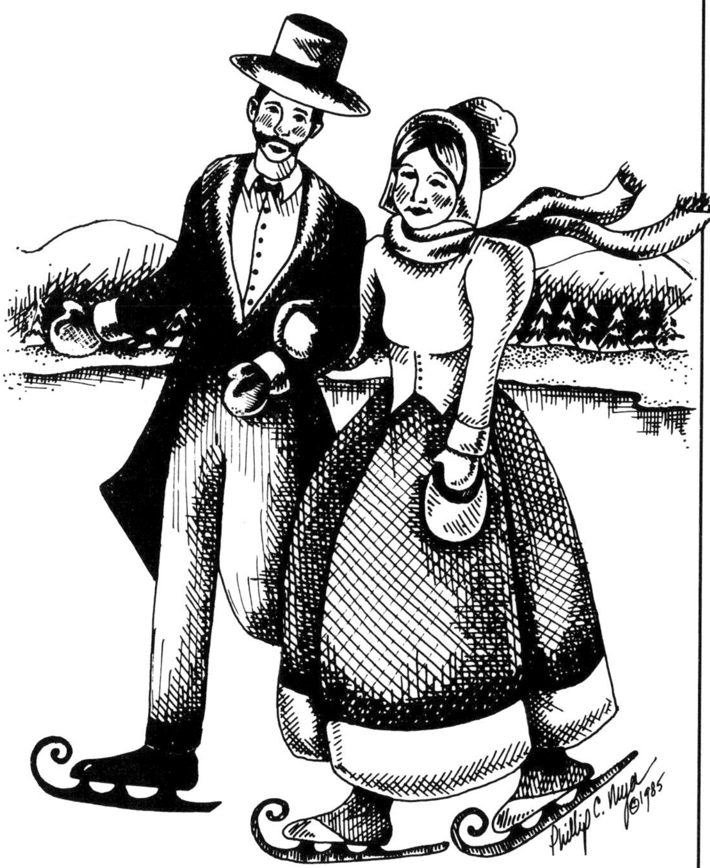

PAINTING INSTRUCTIONS

A. BACKGROUND: *Acrylics*
1. Apply a coat of gesso over the entire plate. Let dry.
2. Trim plate edge with Cornflower Blue.
3. Trace and transfer design to plate.

B. SKY: *Acrylics*
1. BASE sky area in a mixture of Titanium White plus Chrome Oxide Green plus Paynes Gray.
2. Side load a brush with Titanium White and stroke on cloud shapes.

C. BACKGROUND: *Acrylics*
1. BASE mountains on with a mixture of Titanium White plus Paynes Gray.
2. Shade mountain shapes in Paynes Gray washes.
3. HIGHLIGHT with a dry brush of Titanium White.
4. Background trees are painted in a BASE of Chrome Oxide Green plus Black.
5. HIGHLIGHT tree shapes with Titanium White plus Paynes Gray.

D. SNOW and CHURCH: *Acrylics*
1. BASE snow in a coat of Titanium White
2. SHADE with sky mixture.
3. ACCENT with Paynes Gray mixture.

E. LAKE: *Acrylics*
1. BASE frozen lake in sky mixture.
2. SHADE with Paynes Gray wash.
3. HIGHLIGHT with Titanium White.

F. GENTLEMAN SKATER: *Acrylics*
1. Base his jacket, skates, hat rim, and gloves in Black. HIGHLIGHT in White.
2. Paint hat, lapels, and pants in mid value mixture of Paynes Gray plus Titanium White. SHADE with a Black wash HIGHLIGHT with White.
3. Shirt is painted in White, SHADE in Black.
4. Face is painted in flesh mixture of Titanium White plus Burnt Sienna plus Cadmium Red Light.
5. Hair and facial features are painted in Burnt Sienna. ACCENT in Black.

G. LADY SKATER: *Acrylics*
1. Her clothing is painted in two shades of pink, a middle value and a light value made from Alizarin Crimson plus Titanium White.
2. SHADE with a side load of Alizarin Crimson.
3. HIGHLIGHT with a dry brush of Titanium White.
4. Face is painted in flesh mixture of Titanium White plus Burnt Sienna plus Cadmium Red Light.
5. Hair and facial features are painted in Burnt Sienna. ACCENT in Black.
6. Apply rosy cheeks in Cadmium Red Light.

H. GLAZING: *Oils*
1. GLAZE outer edges of plate surface with Burnt Umber oil color. Let dry.
2. Antique entire plate with Burnt Umber.

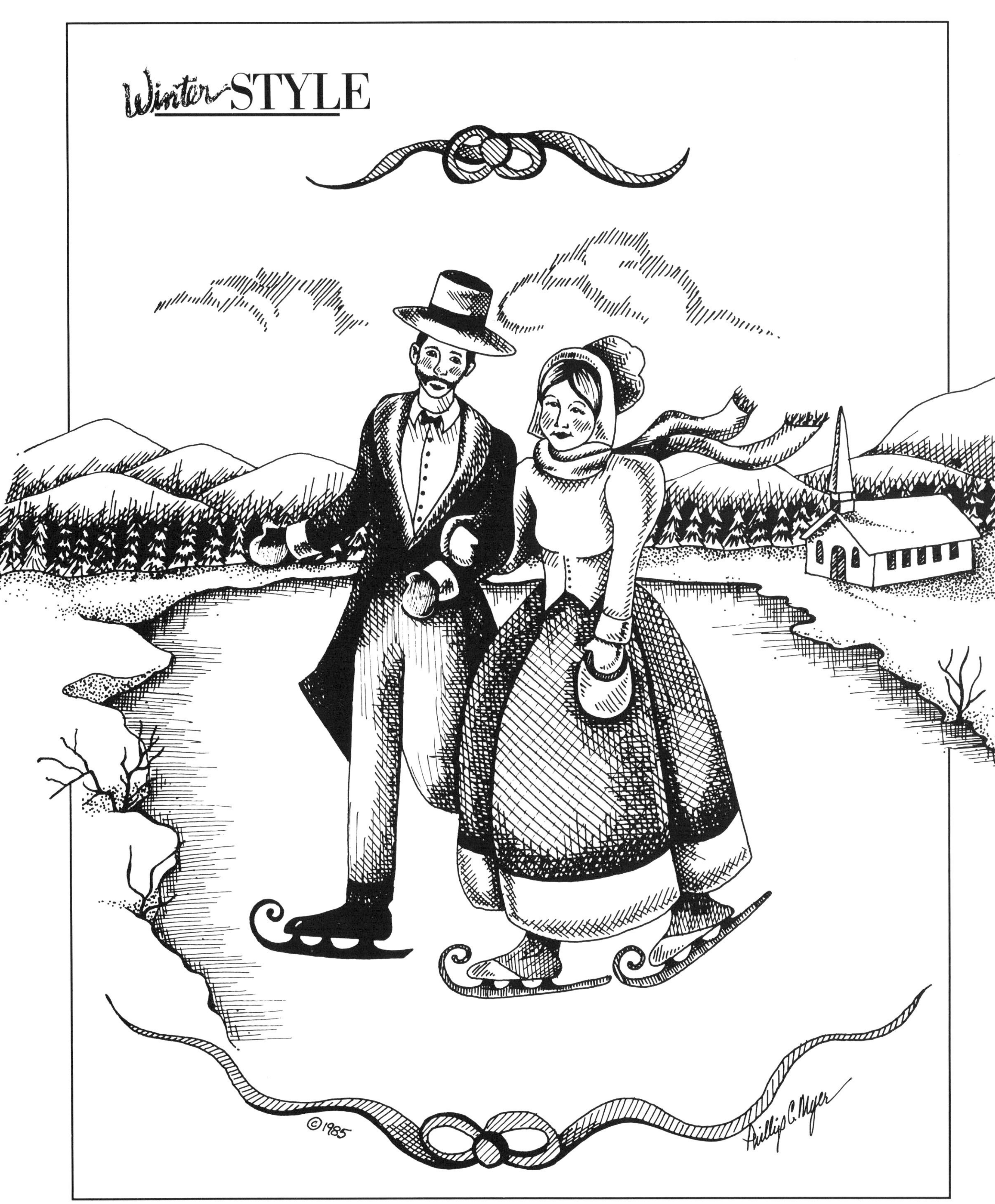
Winter STYLE
©1985

Country STYLE

WEATHERVANE ROOSTER & CAT

Original in the collection of Bruce A. Atzer.

SURFACE: 8″ x 12″ wooden cut outs.

PALETTE: **Permalba Artists' Acrylics:** Bright Red, Mars Black, Cerulean Blue, Titanium White, Yellow Ochre, Burnt Sienna, Burnt Umber, Chrome Oxide Green, Cadmium Yellow Medium, and Alizarin Crimson. **Permalba Artists' Oils:** Asphaltum, Burnt Sienna, Burnt Umber, and Ivory Black.

PAINTING INSTRUCTIONS

A. BACKGROUND: *Acrylics*
1. Prime cut outs with gesso to seal.
2. Sand lightly, trace, and transfer design.

B. ROOSTER: *Acrylics*
1. Comb and waddle are painted in Bright Red. SHADE with a Black wash.
2. BASE head to lower neck in Cerulean Blue plus White. Overstroke with Yellow Ochre then White long feather strokes. Cheek is painted in Yellow Ochre. HIGHLIGHT with White. Eye is painted Black with White HIGHLIGHT.
3. Beak is painted in Yellow Ochre. SHADE with Burnt Sienna.
4. Lower breast area is painted in a mixture of Yellow Ochre plus Burnt Sienna. White dot markings are added.
5. BASE wing in Yellow Ochre. Overstroke with Cadmium Yellow Medium and White brush strokes.
6. Tail feathers are painted in various colors as follows: Bright Red, Chrome Oxide Green, Yellow Ochre, Cadmium Yellow Medium, Cerulean Blue, Titanium White, and Mars Black.
7. Arrow is painted in a mixture of Alizarin Crimson plus Burnt Umber. Stand is painted in a mixture of Cerulean Blue plus White.

C. GLAZING: *Oils*
1. GLAZE rooster sections with a side loaded brush of Burnt Umber plus Black oil colors. Blend with a mop brush. Let dry.
2. Antique entire piece with Burnt Umber oil color.

D. CAT: *Acrylics*
1. BASE eyes in Cadmium Yellow Medium. Outline in Burnt Sienna then Black. SHADE with Burnt Sienna wash. Paint pupils Black. HIGHLIGHT with White.
2. Create liner markings in rows over cat's body with Burnt Sienna and White mixture.
3. Dry brush dark cat markings in Black plus a touch of White.
4. BASE nose in Bright Red plus White. SHADE with Burnt Sienna. Outline lower area of nose and mouth in Black.

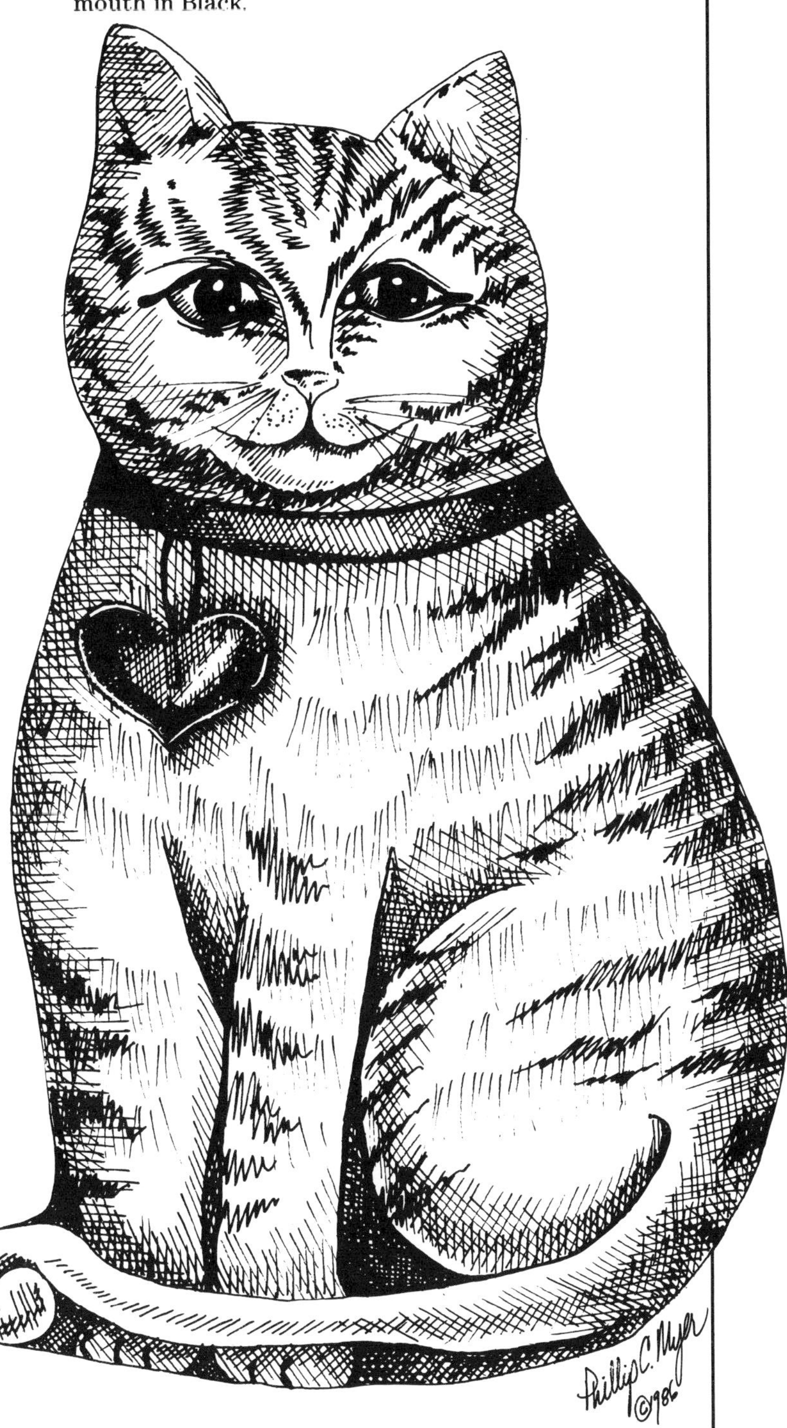

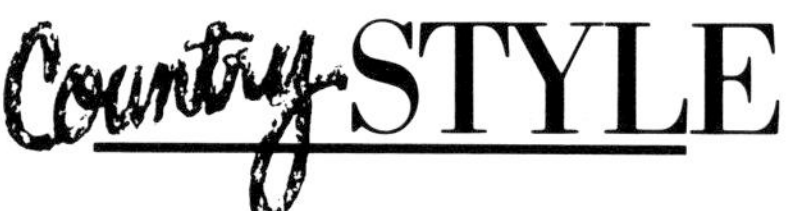

5. Whiskers are painted in a Burnt Umber wash.
6. Various markings around face and ears are painted in Black.
7. Collar is painted in a wash of Black, SHADE with a stronger tone of Black.
8. Hanging heart BASE in Bright Red, SHADE with a Black wash. String is painted in Black.
9. Arrow is painted in Bright Red. Highlight by sanding. Pole is painted Black sanded for HIGHLIGHT. Stand is painted in a mixture of Cerulean Blue plus White.

E. GLAZING: *Oils*
1. GLAZE cat sections with a side loaded brush of Burnt Umber, Asphaltum, Burnt Sienna, and Black. Blend with a mop brush. Let dry.
2. Antique entire piece with Burnt Umber oil color.

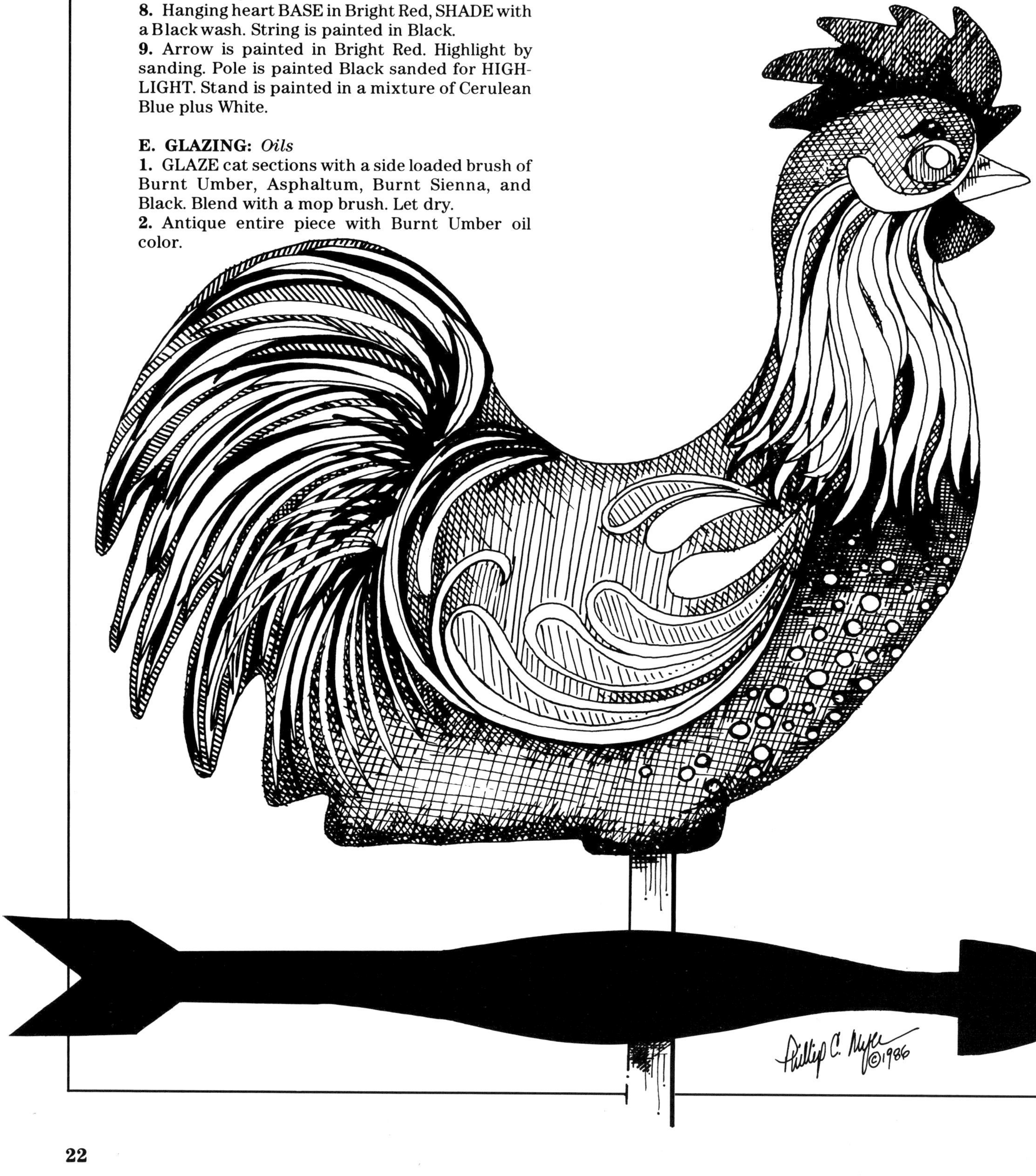

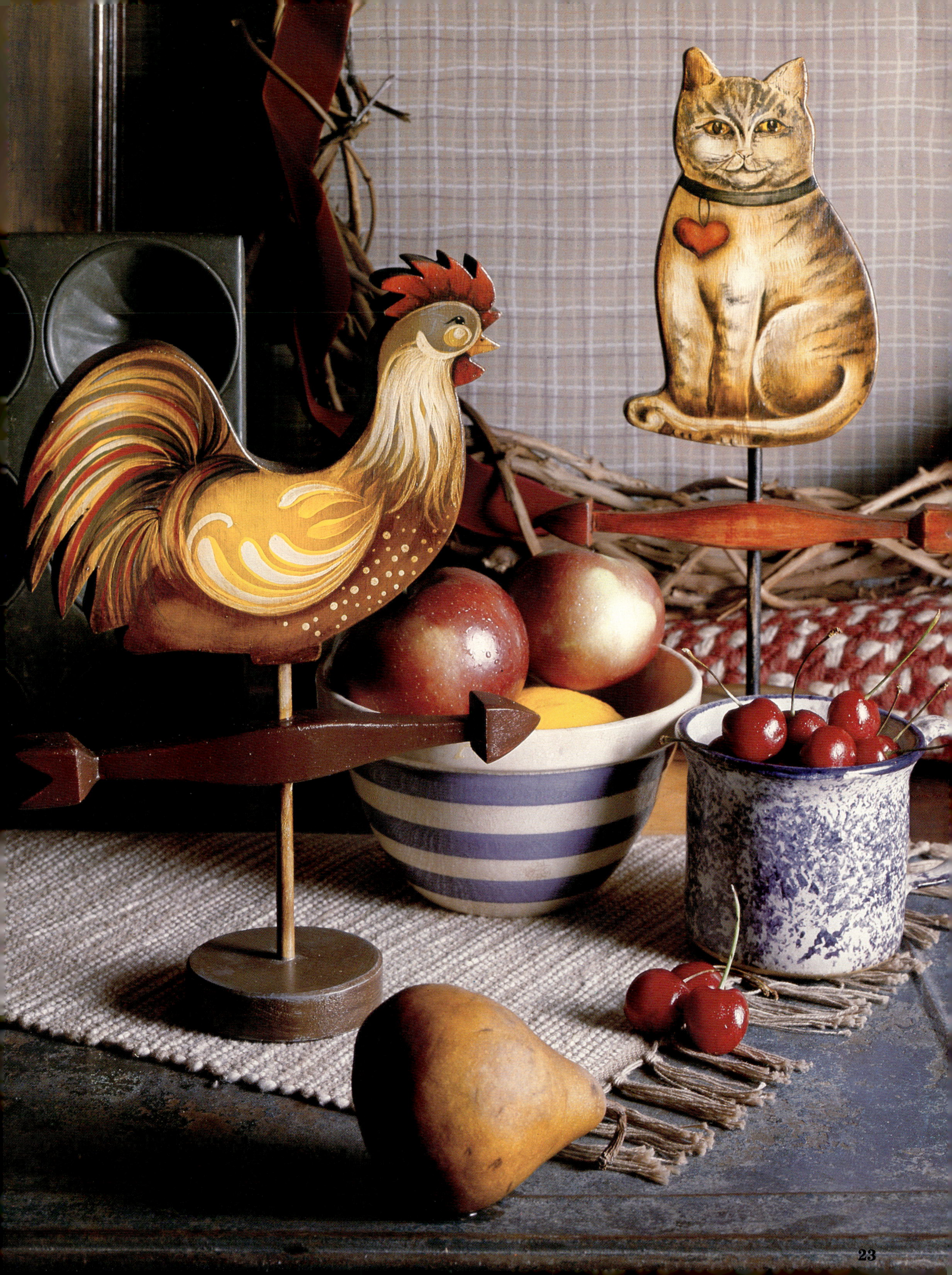

Christmas STYLE

FATHER CHRISTMAS

SURFACE: 12″ x 16″ canvas, 5″ x 10½″ wood cut out or 4″ x 17″ nutcracker.

PALETTE: **Permalba Artists' Acrylics:** Titanium White, Bright Red, Chrome Oxide Green, Mars Black, Burnt Sienna, Paynes Gray, Cadmium Yellow Medium, Burnt Umber, Burnt Sienna, and Cadmium Red Light. **Priscilla Hauser Acrylic:** Malibu. **FolkArt Acrylic:** Barnwood. **Permalba Artists' Oils:** Burnt Umber, Burnt Sienna, Asphaltum, and Ivory Black.

PAINTING INSTRUCTIONS

A. BACKGROUND: *Acrylics*
1. Basecoat entire surface with gesso. Let dry. Apply a second coat.
2. Sand lightly and trace and transfer design.
3. Canvas painting background colors around Father Christmas: Malibu, Barnwood, Bright Red, and tree mixture.

B. FACE: *Acrylics*
1. BASE face area in a mixutre of Titanium White plus Burnt Sienna plus Cadmium Red Light.
2. Lightly sketch face features or transfer.
3. Side load with flesh mixture and a little Cadmium Red Light to SHADE cheek areas, lower nose area, and mouth.
4. Add detail lines around nose, cheek and mouth areas in Burnt Sienna.
5. BASE eyes in Titanium White, paint iris in a mixture of Paynes Gray plus Titanium White. Base pupil in Paynes Gray, HIGHLIGHT in Titanium White.
6. Outline eyes in grey mixture and Paynes Gray straight.

C. BEARD & HAIR: *Acrylics*
1. BASE beard and hair areas in Titanium White.
2. Outline and detail with a light grey mixture creating curls and curving strokes.

D. COAT & HAT: *Acrylics:*
1. BASE red areas (main sections) of coat and hat in Bright Red.
2. BASE coat and hat trim in Titanium White.
3. Side load a flat brush with Mars Black and SHADE coat and hat areas.
4. Trim and detail hat rim with Paynes Gray.
5. Base jingle bell in Cadmium Yellow Medium, SHADE in Burnt Sienna.

E. CHRISTMAS TREE: *Acrylics*
1. BASE tree in mixture of Chrome Oxide Green plus Black.
2. BASE tree trunk in Burnt Sienna.
3. SHADE both sections with a side load of Mars Black.

F. GLOVES: *Acrylics*
1. BASE gloves in a middle value grey made from Paynes Gray plus Titanium White.
2. SHADE with a side load of Paynes Gray.

G. BOOTS: *Acrylics*
BASE in Mars Black.

H. PRESENTS SACK: *Acrylics*
1. BASE sack in a mixture of Titanium White plus Burnt Sienna.
2. SHADE with a wash of Burnt Sienna.
3. ACCENT with a wash of Mars Black.
4. Rope is painted in Black.

I. TOYS: *Acrylics*
1. BASE bear in a mixture of Burnt Umber plus Black.
2. Paint light sections (inner ear sections, paw pad and nose area) in a mixture of base tone plus White.
3. Outline and detail with Mars Black.
4. BASE doll in the following colors: Hair - Cadmium Yellow Medium, Face - flesh mixture, Dress - pink mixture (Bright Red plus White).
5. Outline and detail hair with Burnt Sienna.
6. Face features are painted in Burnt Sienna with Mars Black for eyes and a Bright Red wash for cheeks.

J. BASE STAND: *Acrylics*
BASE in a burgundy tone made from Bright Red plus Burnt Sienna.

K. HIGHLIGHTS:
All highlights on Father Christmas are completed by sanding down to the base. Create this effect by:
1. Choose a medium to coarse grade of sandpaper.
2. Using the sandpaper wrapped around a couple of fingers, sand in light areas (center area of a given section).
3. Sand on the hard side to remove top coats of color, allowing white gesso base to show through, creating a HIGHLIGHT. Remove sanding dust.

L. GLAZING: *Oils*
1. GLAZE SHADE areas with a side load of touches of Burnt Umber, Burnt Sienna, Asphaltum, and Ivory Black.
2. Blend with a mop brush.

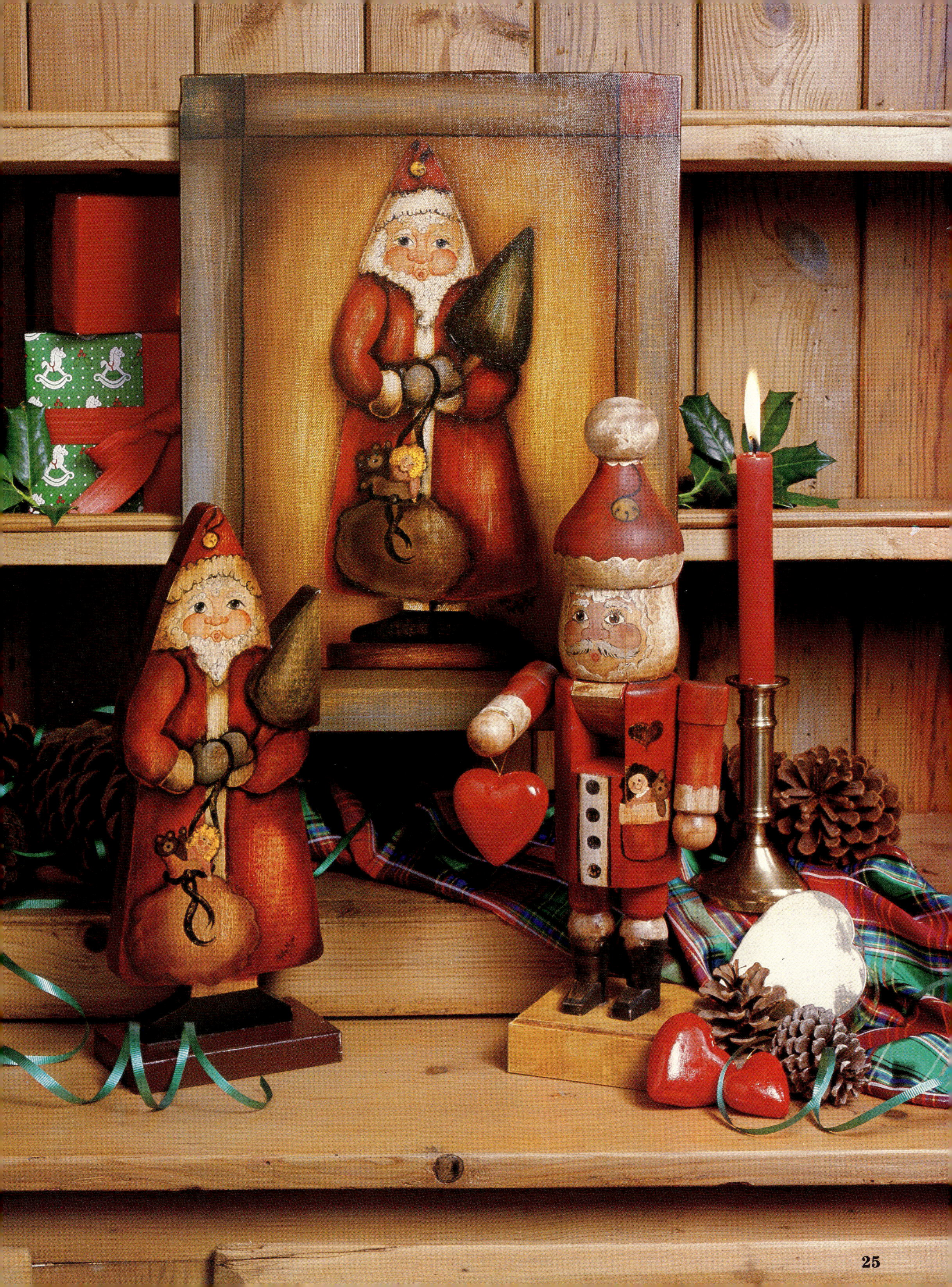

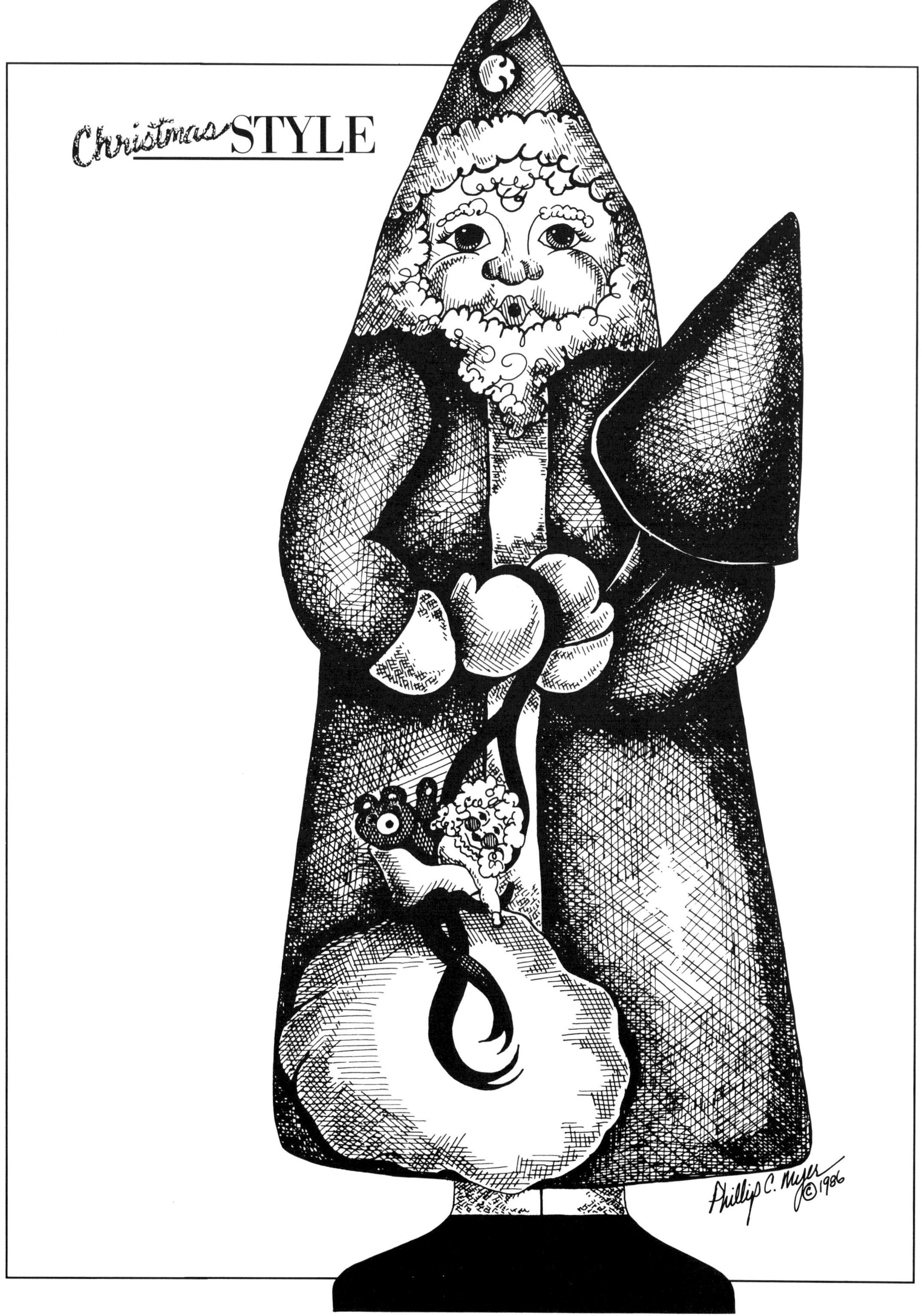
Christmas STYLE
Phillip C. Myer ©1986

Family STYLE

A FOLK ART CHRISTMAS

Original in the collection of Caroline and Anthony Myer.

SURFACE: 12″ round wooden plate.

PALETTE: **Permalba Artists' Acrylics** Paynes Gray, Bright Red, Titanium White, Yellow Ochre, Burnt Sienna, Cadmium Yellow Medium, Chrome Oxide Green, Mars Black, Unbleached Titanium, Alizarin Crimson, **Permalba Artists' Oils:** Burnt Umber and Ivory Black.

PAINTING INSTRUCTIONS:

A. BACKGROUND: *Acrylics*
1. Basecoat entire plate in several coats of gesso.
2. Trim plate edge in a light wash of Bright Red.
3. Overcoat trim edge in a deep blue or color of choice.
4. Trace and transfer pattern design.

B. FIREPLACE: *Acrylics*
1. Base stone area of fireplace in a mixture of Paynes Gray plus White. Overpaint stone shapes in White,White plus Burnt Sienna. SHADE area with Paynes Gray wash.
2. BASE mantle area in Yellow Ochre, SHADE with Burnt Sienna.
3. Baskets and duck decoy on mantle are painted in Yellow Ochre. SHADE with Burnt Sienna and Black.
4. Pewterware on mantle BASE in a mid value shade of gray. SHADE with Paynes Gray, HIGHLIGHT with Titanium White.
5. Ironware in fireplace is painted Black. Firewood BASE in Burnt Sienna, SHADE with Black. Flames BASE in Bright Red wash with a Cadmium Yellow Medium HIGHLIGHT.

C. FLOORBOARDS: *Acrylics*
1. BASE entire floorboard area in Yellow Ochre. Let dry.
2. Pattern transfer board lines if needed.
3. Side load a flat brush with Black and Burnt Sienna, stroke down each board on the left side.

D. CHRISTMAS TREE: *Acrylics*
1. BASE in a mixture of Chrome Oxide Green plus Black. Highlight tips of tree with liner strokes of Chrome Oxide Green plus White.
2. Place garland on with dibs and dabs of Titanium White and Bright Red.
3. Christmas packages are painted various colors,

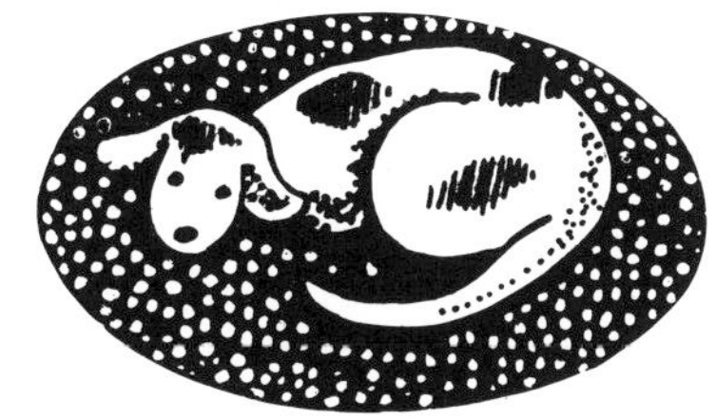

trimmed with those SHADE under packages with a Black wash.

E. OVAL RUG: *Acrylics*
1. BASE entire rug in Mars Black.
2. Place alternating row of Red Oxide, Chrome Oxide Green, Unbleached Titanium, Burnt Sienna, and Yellow Ochre in a dabbing application.

F. FAMILY MEMBERS: *Acrylics*
1. BASE all face and hand features in a flesh mixture of Titanium White plus Burnt Sienna plus Cadmium Red Light.
2. SHADE and outline all face features in Burnt Sienna.
3. SHADE cheeks with a light Alizarin Crimson plus Cadmium Red Light wash. Allow female members to have rosier cheeks.
4. Paint eye shapes and lashes in Black. HIGHLIGHT in White.
5. HAIR: Little boy and girl - BASE in Burnt Umber. SHADE with Black, Mother - BASE in Black, SHADE with BLACK plus White, Father - BASE in Burnt Sienna, SHADE in Burnt Umber, Baby - BASE in a light Burnt Sienna wash.
6. Mother, baby and little girl are painted in various shades of blue clothing. Create value mixtures from Phthalo Blue, Titanium White, and Black. Shade with a Black wash. Mother's apron -BASE in White, SHADE with Black wash.
7. Little boy's clothing is painted in green shades made from Chrome Oxide Green plus White. SHADE with Black.
8. Father's clothing is painted in Yellow Ochre and Burnt Sienna. SHADE with Burnt Sienna and Black.
9. Dog BASE in Unbleached Titanium, SHADE with Burnt Sienna and Black. Spots are painted in a Burnt Sienna wash.
10. Little girl's doll is painted in pinks, use Alizarin Crimson plus White. SHADE and detail with Burnt Sienna.

G. DETAILS: *Acrylics*
1. Sand HIGHLIGHT into plate edge area. This will bring out underneath color.
2. Apply banner areas on plate with a light wash of color in Black. Let dry. Sand HIGHLIGHT.
3. Lettering on banner is applied with thin White.

H. GLAZING: *Oils*
1. Side load with Black and Burnt Umber oil colors. Place this tone in all SHADE areas. Blend with mop brush to soften. Let dry.
2. Antique entire plate with a Burnt Umber glaze.

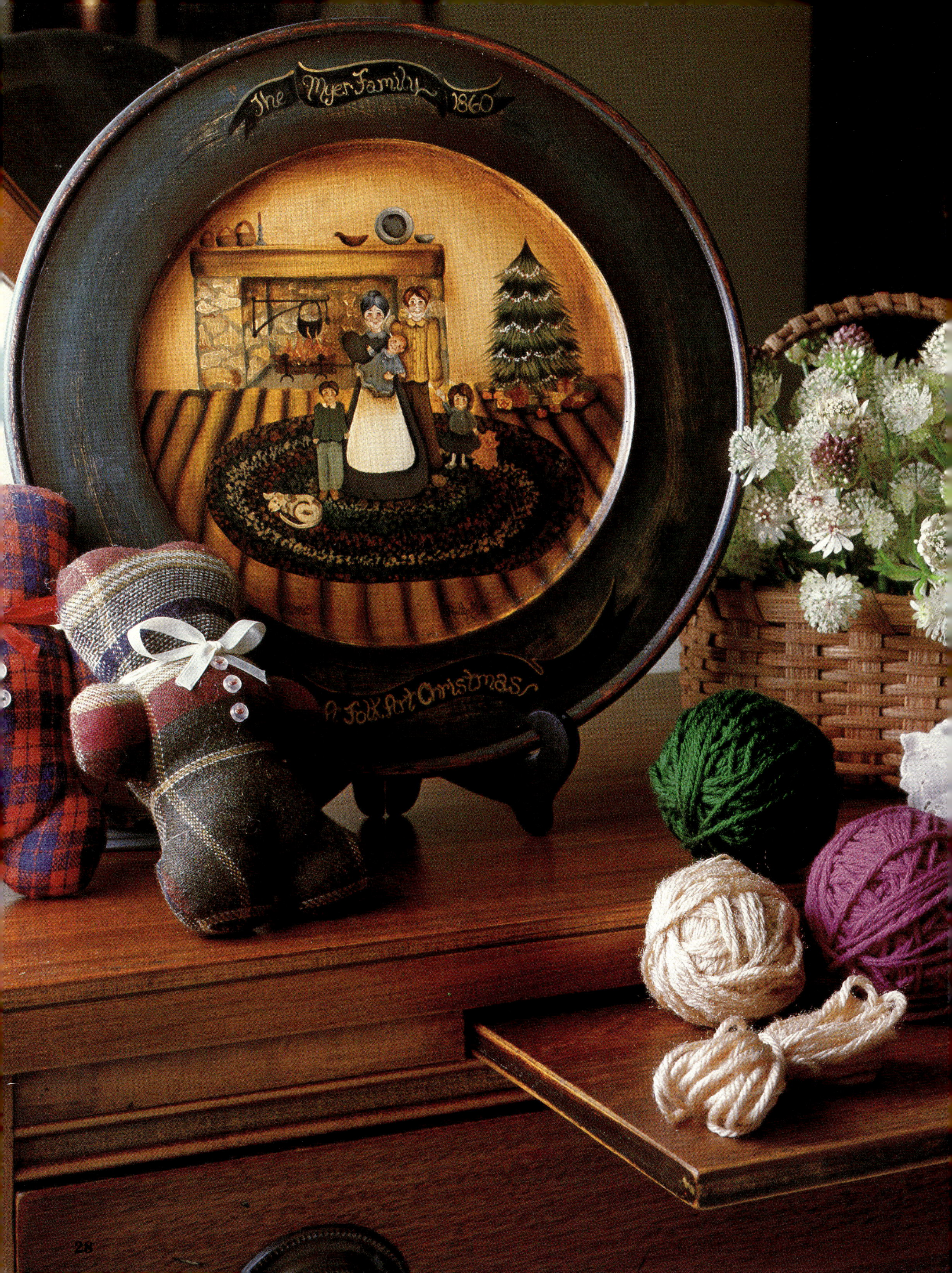
The Myer Family 1860
A Folk Art Christmas

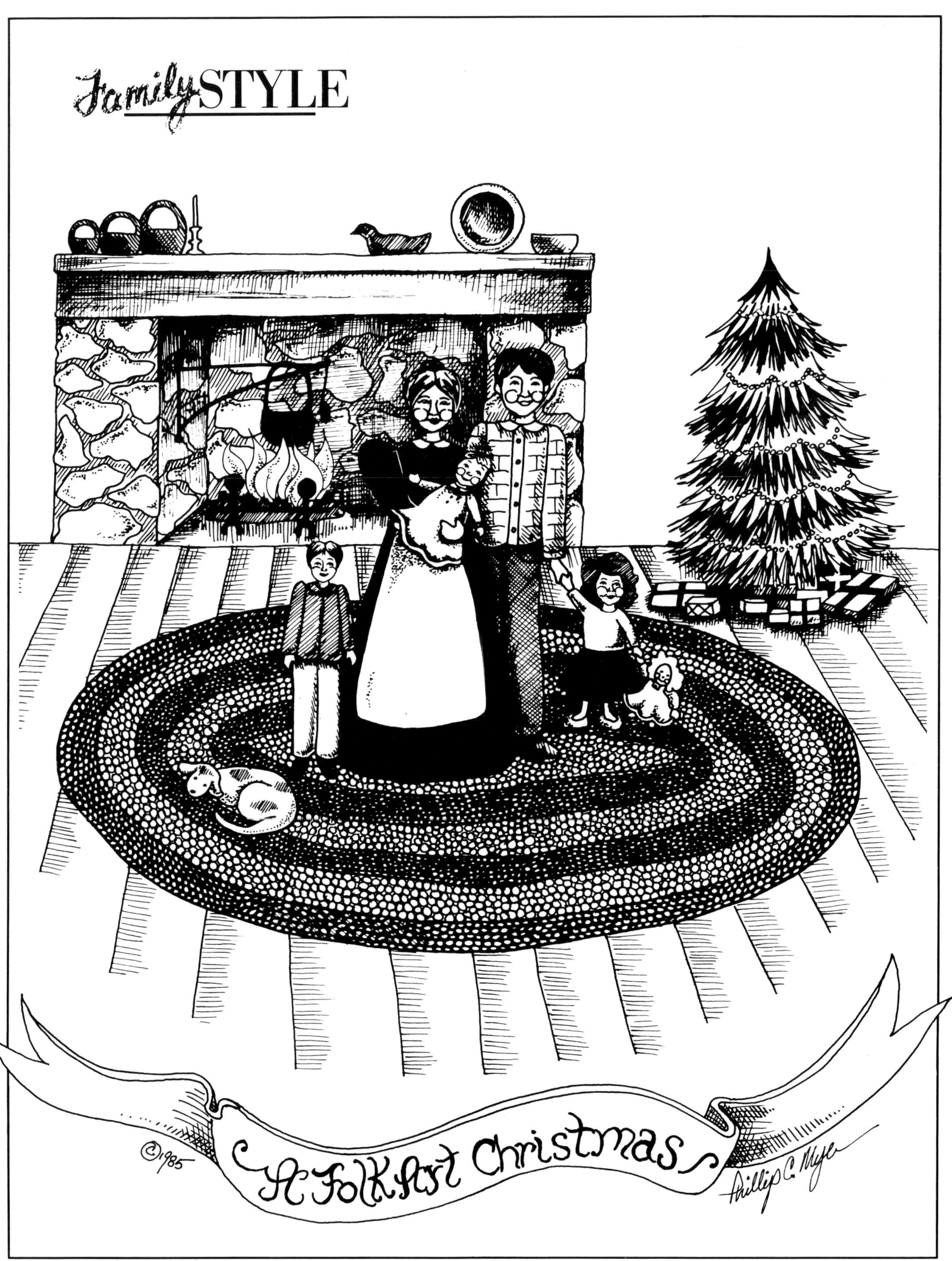

Family STYLE
A Folk Art Christmas
©1985
Phillip C. Myer

Heart STYLE

A FRUIT BOWL OF PLENTY

SURFACE: 10¾″ x 16¾″ wooden tin board.

PALETTE: **Permalba Artists' Acrylics:** Alizarin Crimson, Burnt Sienna, Bright Red, Burnt Umber, Cadmium Red Light, Cadmium Yellow Medium, Chrome Oxide Green, Cobalt Blue, Hansa Yellow Light, Mars Black, Titanium White, and Yellow Ochre. **Permalba Artists' Oils:** Asphaltum, Burnt Umber, Burnt Sienna, and Ivory Black.

PAINTING INSTRUCTIONS

A. BACKGROUND: *Acrylics*
1. Punch tin design with hammer and punch tool or awl.
2. BASE the entire fruit design area in a coat of Titanium White acrylic color with a large Flat brush. Apply a second coat once the first has completely dried.
3. Pattern transfer the section lines between pieces of fruit. No detail lines are necessary.
4. Now, BASE in each fruit section with a coat of its corresponding acrylic base tone. Pineapple: Yellow Ochre, Pineapple Blades: Chrome Oxide Green plus Mars Black, Apple: Bright Red, Peach: Cadmium Yellow Medium, Grapes: Cobalt Blue plus Mars Black and DO NOT BASE in the strawberries at this time leave White basecoat.
5. Apply a second coat once first application of color has dried.

B. PINEAPPLE: *Acrylics*
1. Pattern transfer the individual sections on the pineapple body area.
2. Side load a flat brush with Burnt Sienna and SHADE bottom of section which form "U"'s.
3. Restroke with Sienna to strengthen.
4. Highlight only mid right hand section with a side load of a mixture of Titanium White plus Yellow Ochre.
5. Accent a few tips in HIGHLIGHT area with Titanium White.
6. Apply a WASH of Burnt Sienna down left hand and lower side of pineapple. Let dry.
7. Apply a WASH of Burnt Umber in same area.

C. PINEAPPLE BLADES: *Acrylics*
1. Pattern transfer blade sections with White chalk.
2. SHADE bottom area of blades with Mars Black.
3. Side load a flat brush with Hansa Yellow Light and HIGHLIGHT some center blade tips.

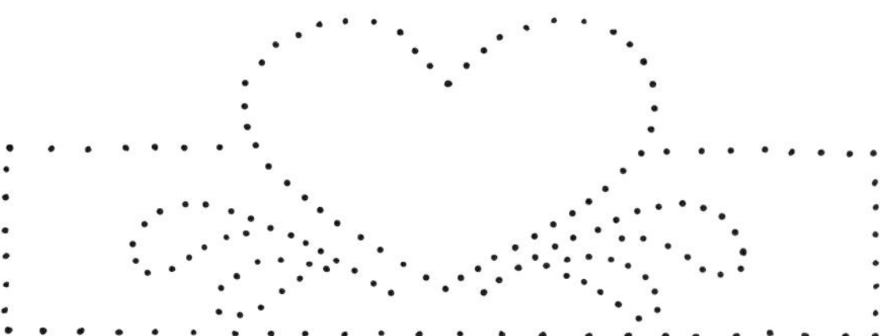

D. APPLE: *Acrylics*
1. SHADE lower area of apple in WASHES of Burnt Umber and Alizarin Crimson.
2. Stroke dark shading colors on with a liner brush for texture marks.
3. HIGHLIGHT separately with Cadmium Red Light, Cadmium Yellow Medium, and Titanium White.
4. Stem is painted in Burnt Umber, HIGHLIGHTED with Titanium White.

E. PEACH: *Acrylics*
1. Dry brush a mixture of Alizarin Crimson plus a touch of Burnt Umber to the "C" area and crack area. Build up slowly.
2. HIGHLIGHT areas are dry brushed with Titanium White.

F. STRAWBERRIES: *Acrylics*
1. Side load a flat brush with Bright Red and SHADE outer edge. Leave White for HIGHLIGHT area.
2. SHADE with a side loaded of Alizarin Crimson plus Burnt Umber.
3. Seeds are painted with Cadmium Yellow Medium and accented with Mars Black.
4. Strawberry bracts are BASED in dark green mix, HIGHLIGHTED with Hansa Yellow Light.

G. GRAPES: *Acrylics*
1. Create a lighter shade of blue from base tone mixture by adding Titanium White. BASE in light and mid value area of grapes leaving a "C" of dark base showing.
2. Outline top right side of each grape with a lighter blue mix.
3. ACCENT bottom left side with a mixture of Cadmium Red Light plus White.
4. HIGHLIGHT with Titanium White dashes.

H. GLAZING: *Oils*
1. Glaze the fruit in combinations of the following colors: Asphaltum, Burnt Sienna, Burnt Umber, and Ivory Black.
2. Blend and soften with a mop brush.

I. DETAILS: *Oils*
1. After the piece is thoroughly dry, antique with a mixture of Burnt Umber plus a touch of Burnt Sienna.
2. Stripe edge of board with Black using a striper or liner brush.

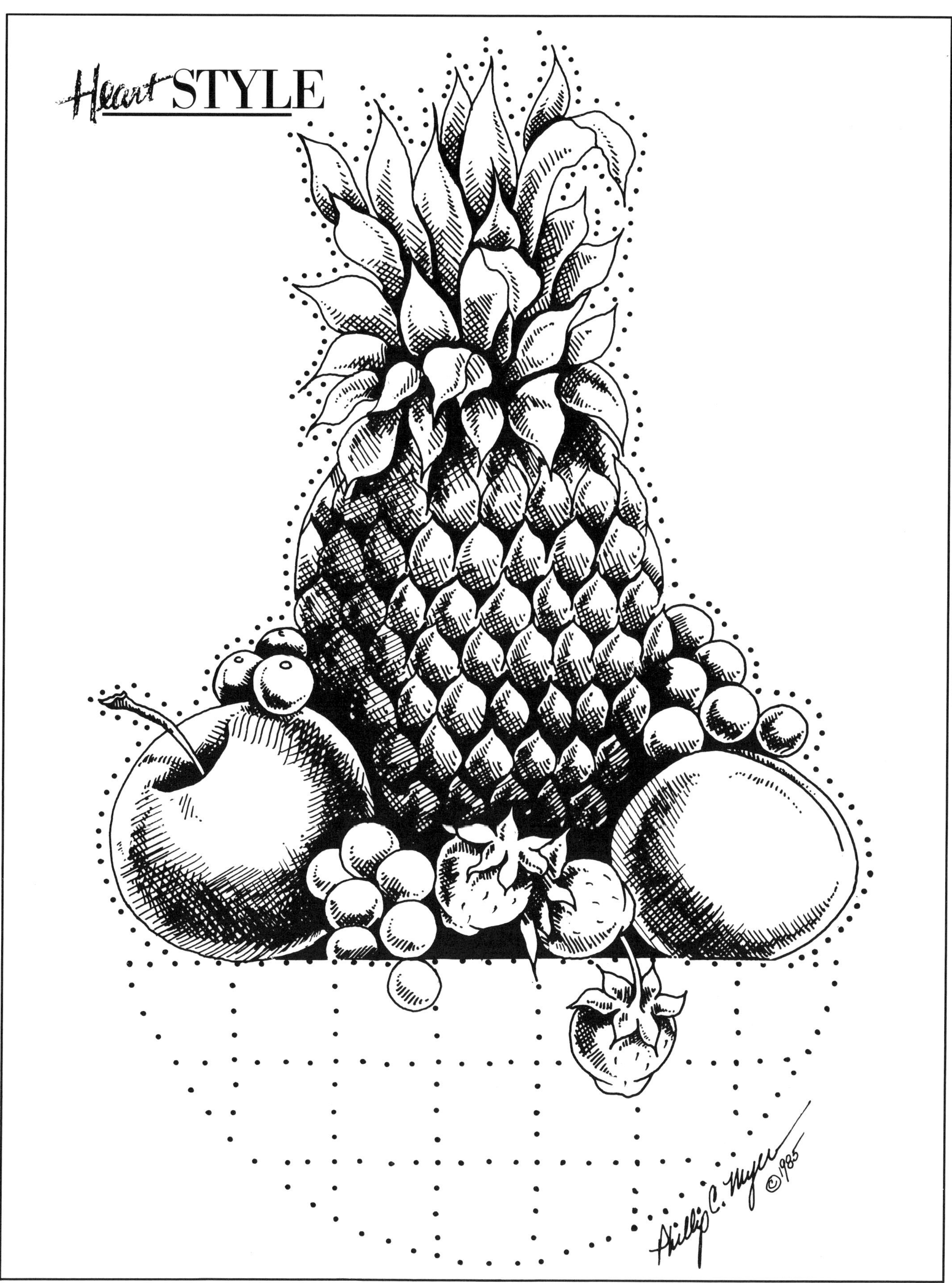
Heart STYLE
Phillip C. Myer ©1985

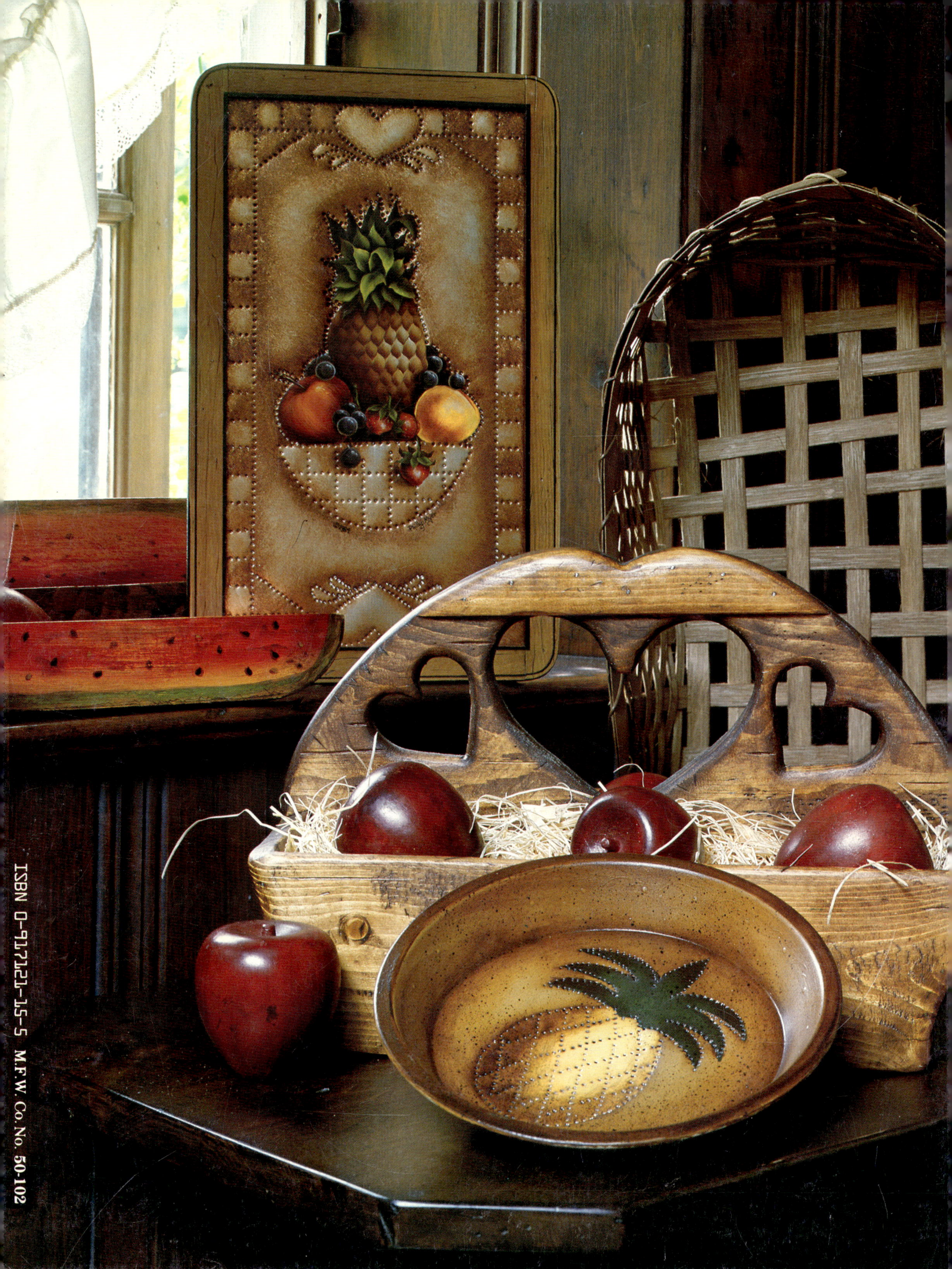

ISBN 0-917121-15-5 M.F.W. Co. No. 50-102